TOWARD
A NEW MUSIC

Da Capo Press Music Reprint Series

GENERAL EDITOR
ROLAND JACKSON

TOWARD
A NEW MUSIC

Music and Electricity

By

CARLOS CHAVEZ

Translated from the Spanish by Herbert Weinstock

DA CAPO PRESS • NEW YORK • 1975

Library of Congress Cataloging in Publication Data

Chávez, Carlos, 1899-
Toward a new music.

(Da Capo Press music reprint series)
Reprint of the 1937 ed. published by Norton, New
York.
1. Musical instruments, Electronic. 2. Music—
History and criticism—20th century. 3. Music—
Acoustics and physics. 4. Moving-pictures, Musical.
I. Weinstock, Herbert, 1905-1971, tr. II. Title.
ML1092.C45 1975   789.9   74-28308
ISBN 0-306-70719-5

This Da Capo Press edition of *Toward a New Music* is an unabridged
republication of the first edition published in New York in 1937.
It is reprinted with the permission of W. W. Norton & Company.

Published by Da Capo Press, Inc.
A Subsidiary of Plenum Publishing Corporation
227 West 17th Street, New York, N.Y. 10011

TOWARD A NEW MUSIC
Music and Electricity

TOWARD A NEW MUSIC

Music and Electricity

By CARLOS CHAVEZ

Translated from the Spanish by Herbert Weinstock

With eight illustrations by Antonio Ruíz

W. W. NORTON & COMPANY, INC.
Publishers   *New York*

First Edition

Contents

FOREWORD BY THE TRANSLATOR 7

1. SEEING THE PRESENT IN PERSPEC-
   TIVE 13

2. MUSIC AND PHYSICS 17

3. MUSICAL PRODUCTION AND REPRO-
   DUCTION 26

4. ELECTRIC INSTRUMENTS OF MUSI-
   CAL REPRODUCTION 41

5. THE SOUND FILM 89

6. THE RADIO 122

7. ELECTRIC APPARATUS OF SOUND
   PRODUCTION 138

8. TOWARD A NEW MUSIC 166

Foreword by the Translator

~~~~~~

CARLOS CHAVEZ was born in the environs of
Mexico City on June 13, 1899. At the age of twelve,
he was reading books on keyed instruments and
chromatic brasses, and thinking about the limitations
imposed on early composers by primitive instruments. By 1918 he was composing a symphony, and
three years later had produced a string quartet
clearly containing the elements of his mature style.
He was beginning to take a leading part in Mexico's
musical life.

Chavez spent the winter of 1923-24 in New York,
and was fascinated by the radio's first uncertain steps
outside the laboratory. Here was an instrument offering immense new resources to composers. From that
time on, his interest in electric instruments has increased. He did not have to make time in which to
gather the material for the chapters that follow.
Every act of his life as a musician has led him to the
subject, provided him with exactly this material.
His motivating belief in music as a human necessity,

a true social good, which has led him to compose, conduct, and educate, made this book inevitable. It is another natural expression of a completely integrated human being.

In July, 1928, Chavez became conductor of the orchestra of Mexico City's musicians' union. In nine years of unremitting effort he has transformed it into the excellent Symphony Orchestra of Mexico. He has served as Director of the National Conservatory of Music and Chief of the Department of Fine Arts of the Secretariat of Public Education. He has continued to compose.

In 1932, Leopold Stokowski conducted the world premier of Chavez' ballet, *H. P.*, in Philadelphia. Chavez made his third visit to the United States, and Stokowski took him to visit the R. C. A.-Victor studios in Camden and the Bell Telephone laboratories in New York. Because of his continuing interest in the musical potentialities of electric communication and sound reproduction, Chavez had been commissioned by the Secretary of Public Education to make a report on their latest developments in the United States. That report, which appeared serially in *El Universal* of Mexico City in July and August, 1932, was the genesis of *Toward a New Music*.

Since 1918, Carlos Chavez has been waging an uninterrupted and winning fight for the cause of living music in Mexico. His growing fame in the United States has brought about a widening of his activities, for which those who do not believe that music came to an end in *Tristan*—or *Le Sacre*—should be grateful. In the past two years he has been guest conductor of the Philadelphia, Boston, and New York Philharmonic orchestras.

This book is as truly contemporary, as firmly founded on reality, as *H. P.*, the *Sinfonia de Antigona*, the *Sinfonia India*, and the other compositions which Chavez has added to the literature of really living music. It is a statement of faith in art as a continuously unfolding process, in human beings, and in science. It is a gesture of gratitude to the inventors and engineers who have been producing for music the richest instrumental resources it has ever had. Most important of all, it is an invitation to musicians, and to composers in particular, to take advantage of the techniques at hand in their task of making a music germane to our day. If *Toward a New Music* helps to turn the eyes and energies of musicians toward the true musical potentialities of electric instruments, it will have served Carlos Chavez' purpose in writing it.

This translation is in a very real sense a collaboration. Chavez' understanding of English assures me that it exactly conveys the meaning of his Spanish original. My part in it has been one of the most stimulating experiences of my life.

HERBERT WEINSTOCK

New York
January 26, 1937

TOWARD A NEW MUSIC
Music and Electricity

1. Seeing the Present in Perspective

THE present is the clearest reality of life. It is hardly strange, then, that it is the most difficult period for us to observe. We are inside the present, and this very nearness allows us to see only fragments of it. What prevents us from seeing the true contents of the present easily is that very past of which it is so full, of which it is to a large extent made.

We want to see the present as we see a city from an airplane. This may seem paradoxical, because it is impossible to live other than in the present, and equally impossible to have perspective on anything when we are within it. Nevertheless, there is no paradox involved. My contention is that in order to contemplate the present in its context we must go to the past. The future, the present, and the past are three completely distinct times, like three movements of a symphony. They nevertheless connect and continue each other in a manner making it impossible to distinguish between them with complete precision. The problem is to

13

travel in the past knowing that it is over, without confusing it with today.

The past is history. It has often been said that the great masters of music, for example, were ahead of their time. This, I think, is not true. The great masters were not ahead of their time—their public was behind it. The general public likes to live in the past. This is the reason that the composers of yesterday are the recognized artists of today, those of today the artists of tomorrow. The general public is always one bar behind, syncopated, marking an afterbeat. The delay is sometimes of years, even of decades or centuries, but it always exists. The good artist is related to his time, and so is his art—which, however, will become useful to the public in general only in some more or less distant future.

The explanation is very simple: it is easy to retrace the highroad already constructed, but very difficult to build new roads, to project and clear new routes. Furthermore, the present is full of remnants of the past which, by resisting the onward movement of time, have unmistakably proved their validity. The past is thus undergoing a constant process of selection. It is because of all these things that to accept the marvelous art of the European classics as our own truths, already worked out, is comfortable and pleasant. To seek new forms of expression for the uncertainties and needs of our own period is arduous.

The first way conduces to peace, repose, and contemplation; the second incites to motion, struggle, and discovery. The great classic composers, each in his own epoch, chose movement, struggle, and discovery. That is why there has been progress.

Our proposal to see the past as such does not mean to denigrate—much less to deny—it. It simply means that we shall adopt a line of movement instead of halting to enjoy the contemplation of completed works. Common criticism, on the other hand, does denigrate and deny today's possibilities. It calls our time prosaic, vulgar, matter-of-fact, and sees the past as poetic and inspired. It is not easy for the general public to comprehend that an era of electricity and great mechanical inventions may inspire profound works of art, works worthy of being classed with the symphonies of Beethoven and the cantatas of Bach. It is difficult to realize that the great contemporary advance of science will result in a marvelous artistic flowering.

However, a moment's consideration will reveal that any given epoch seemed at the time more prosaic than its predecessor exactly because of its greater material and scientific development. The Periclean age, the Renaissance, and the eighteenth and nineteenth centuries—glorious periods in art—seemed thus prosaic when they were the present. The general notion has always been that the present is commonplace. We must purify this concept, search out a more useful perspective. The present age, with its fertile agitation, its incredible social injustices, its portentous scientific development, is perfecting, in electricity, its own organ of expression, its own voice. This, clarified and matured, will become the legitimate art of our era, the art of today.

I have always thought that an analysis of our present artistic situation and its expressive potentialities must begin with the study of its determining causes, a retrospective study of the development of art in relation to man's domination of physical means. It seems to me, in short, that history and physics will well explain the artistic phenomena of today. Only by their study may we obtain a much-needed perspective on the present, just as a mariner, to confirm his route, must first ascertain his position on the vastness of the ocean.

2. Music and Physics

ALL the arts are presented by means of physical phenomena, physical means. Music uses sound, vibrations. Architecture uses matter: "materials" as they are called in the trade, baked clay, wood, blocks of stone, steel, concrete. Both vibrations and matter, considered separately, have been the subject of studies, and present purely physical characteristics. That is to say, if we study an isolated sound, we undertake a task falling within the disciplines of physics. We see that it possesses physical qualities: *intensity, duration, timbre, pitch.* When we study the materials of architecture, we also encounter physical qualities: resistance, color, elasticity, rigidity, permeability.

Vibrations or physical means when grouped together acquire aesthetic properties. Sounds when joined in a manner dictated by a man's sensitivity and desires are already music, and acquire those meanings and expressions we call artistic. The same thing occurs when we similarly group solid materials

17

—which then become architecture. It is true that the creative imagination may sometimes conceive music in impossible sounds, or sculpture in impossible masses, volumes, and colorings. This merely means that, for the time being, imagination is outdistancing the material means of realization, and cannot yet express itself in artistic terms. No art in the world exists outside physics, and the specific nature of art has therefore always depended, necessarily, on the physical properties of the material used. It is clear that tree-trunks and branches determine a special architecture; cut stone another; wallboard and brick another. One need not go very far to realize the degree to which, in architecture, physical qualities of the materials and man's increasing ability to manage and use them have determined artistic expressions of beauty as singular and diverse as that of a hut of wood and branches, that of a stone cathedral, and that of a steel and concrete skyscraper. Man could not express the strength of his aesthetic conception, or create such formidable architectonic masses as the towers of New York, when the only materials of construction were tree-trunks and branches. When philosophers assure us that there is no progress in art, and that "the work of art is equal to the work of art," we should take refuge in the fact that art depends on physics, and that the physico-mechanical sciences are advancing in the sense of attaining constantly greater extension, freedom, and intensity in the domination of natural elements.

We call a piece of music beautiful when the emotions, feelings, and ideas of the creator approximate those of the listener. This reciprocal expressiveness is as possible in a melody played on a Greek flute with few stops as in one played on a modern flute. They are equal in that both are tubes containing a column of air vibrated at will by the breath. However, the extraordinarily ingenious mechanical system of keys, perfected through the centuries, that we now have, means an infinitely greater command over this column of air than the Greeks had. In musical terminology, this signifies that we have achieved more sounds as well as greater facility and speed in producing them, without sacrificing a single quality of the ancient flute.

Surely progress in the physical and mechanical sciences determines a progress in art, since the artist of today has at his command the resources of yesterday plus many more. Not to have achieved this physico-mechanical progress would have been to perpetuate for centuries a music of extremely narrow resources, in which man's growing need for expression would not have found all the desired means of performance. Man has a growing need for expression and creation, and also the growing capacity to understand natural resources and place them at his disposal. If we do not wish to call the results of the exercise of these human abilities *progress,* we shall be arguing about terms. As I said above, the beauty of art is not an objective quality, but a relative value established between the creator and the public by the greater or lesser affinity of feeling and idea existing between them. The essential quality of art, that is, is the human element it contains. This element is to be found in equal strength in so-called primitive music and in the contemporary music using physico-mechanical developments. Progress is implied when man, to express himself and satisfy his desires, makes use of better, more varied, richer, and more manageable elements.

It is fitting to mention here that the industrial procedures of the present economic system—typified in this case by the tendency toward standardization as a means of obtaining the greatest commercial return—deprive society of the variety of high types of product which human ability is capable of producing. In the construction of many electric musical instruments, for example, I know it to be a fact that the development has been very great. But the commercial types on sale to the public are very inferior to those existing in experimental laboratories.

Let us return to the principal point, and glance at the historical development of music. The general character of art has depended on the physical means for embodying it. Terpander "enriches" Greek music by adding strings to the lyre. Oriental instruments with necks, sound-boxes, and multiple strings invade Europe in the Middle Ages because they bring greater facility of expression. The instrument with a neck signifies nothing less than the material means of developing chromaticism easily, a resource physically impossible on the purely diatonic Greek lyres and flutes. Chromaticism in turn signifies a new source of musical expression. The chromaticism of twelve tones having been established, and the thousand attempts to establish the consequent temper having been made, wind instruments, dormant during the Middle Ages, and still confined to diatonicism, are the object of new attention, of attempts to make them chromatic. The systems of keys and stops begin to develop, and finally the mechanical advance characteristic of the nineteenth century makes it possible to conquer the construction problems of keyed and pistoned instruments, which the artisan of the Middle Ages could not dream of constructing with anvil and hammer.

Instruments depending on compressed air appeared in antiquity. Their possibilities for musical production were determined by the capacity of one man to blow and maintain a reserve of air under pressure. Bagpipes endured long years, long ages, until the day when pipers thought of reserves of air controlled in better ways, progressing with man's better control of material resources, and the great pipe-organ was finally produced—an instrument which is still a marvel of musical expression. Let us remember that an instrument of such gigantic proportions can exist only thanks to the thousand conquests of the physical and constructive sciences, and that the music which can be conceived and created on it is determined by the special and complex domination of sounds which it places at our disposal. The sciences have made possible the development from the bagpipes to the great organ just as in architecture they made possible that from the hut to the skyscraper.

Our epoch, our century, this year, witness a rapid growth in the sciences. The achievements they offer us constitute many new resources for the better satisfaction of our needs of every order, for the greater command of means, and—this is what interests us most here—for the greater facility of expression. Much has been said of the advantages and benefits to man when, thanks to scientific advance, he has been able to produce and take greater advantage of the energies of heat, light, and mechanics, and transform one into another to produce transportation, heating, lighting, and the end-products of industry. But there has been no clear conception of how much the development of physics and mechanics has signified to the progress of the fine arts. The idea that art is a "purely ideal" part of human activity; the idea, defended insistently by philosophers, that there is no progress in art; the small interest which artists and scientists have had in relating the disciplines of art and science closely; all this has resulted in a considerable delay in the true comprehension of art's basis in science as far as its means of existence go.

Concretely, in the field of music, the last fifteen or twenty years have given us, as a scientific advance, electric instruments for musical production and reproduction. We well recognize the importance of central heating, of electric lighting, of rapid transportation by land, water, and air. But we have not recognized, nor given its true valuation to, the production and reproduction of sound by means of electricity. We have not clearly evaluated the significance of the extension and fullness which electric instruments for production and reproduction give our capacity for expression. To understand this well, we must first remember the high significance of expression itself: every man takes into account the benefit he receives when he is cold, and warms himself, but few realize the immense liberation implied in being able to express one's self. Primitive man, closer to the other animals than modern man is, and still suffering many adversities now avoided, understood this, and often thanked his deities for the privilege of an articulated voice. A man and a quadruped are happy when they feel the surrounding warmth they both need, but only man can satisfy the imperative need for expression through a means as eloquent as language or art. Substantially, the inferiority of the animal with respect to man is rooted in its deficiency of expression.

The electric apparatus of sound production and reproduction augment extraordinarily the range and capacity of our expression. Perhaps we are too close to their discovery to see their transcendent importance in art and in human culture in general. It was only a few years ago that "celebrated artists" considered playing or singing on the radio a lesser function which did not square with their lofty position; even some of the commercial firms now handling the radio began by denying its value, or accepted it tardily. At the present time, it must be noted that the blame for bad broadcasts has nothing to do with the radio itself as a means of reproducing and spreading sound. Only a small effort of imagination is required to enable us to envisage the time when the radio (to mention only one of the electric apparatus of musical reproduction) may transform radically or completely replace institutions now seeming to us as solid as the daily paper, the book and magazine, the concert, the theater, and—more than anything—the school in all its grades.

As regards electric instruments for producing sound, the enmity with which the few musicians who know them regard them is manifest. These judge them superficially, consider them ugly, of small practical value, unnecessary. The public, the great public, does not know them, and knows very little of their existence. Little that is favorable to their artistic development can be said with reference to the direction taken by their inventors and the few others directly interested in them. These people undiscerningly want the new electric instruments to imitate the instruments now in use as faithfully as possible and to serve the music we already have.

What is needed is an understanding of all the physical possibilities of the new instruments. We must clearly evaluate the increase they bring to our own capacity for expression and the magnitude of the advance they make possible in satisfying man's supreme need for communication with his fellows.

3. Musical Production and Reproduction

~~~~~~~~~~~~~~~~~~~~~~~~~~~~~~~~~~~~~~

Musical Production

WE ought to deduce the necessity of producing music from the fundamental conditions of human nature. Thought and feeling are the superior functions of man, but we should also observe that what is thought and felt implies and determines the need to express.

The interdependence of thought and its expression is, without doubt, one of the richest and most interesting subjects for study. But in this book I wish to refer only to the important fact of this interdependence and its most obvious consequence: that the faculty of thinking and feeling obliges the individual to search for and find an adequate form of expression, and that the efficacy and manner of this form of expression directly influence thought and feeling themselves, giving them a particular character.

The highest degree of development man's intelligence (as contrasted with that of the so-called inferior animals) has achieved is in his capacity for articulated language and art, the two great means of expression—which the other animals either lack, or have just begun to develop—and in all that these signify in the development of the moral, aesthetic, and social sense of the individual. Man's intelligence, while developing in itself, has been making a parallel development of the necessary organs of expression, which, in turn, correlatively assist its unfolding.

Articulated language and the fine arts are the means of expression man has been developing through the ages in relation to the evolution of his thought and feeling. The articulated word has been used for more ordinary and private expressions, music for more abstract ones. Man's ancestors shouted, groaned, laughed, before arriving at articulated language. The cries, groans, laughs, the modulations of the voice, which preceded the word, were in reality music. Music existed before actual words, and the man of today instinctively makes his common speech more musical, more accented and rhythmic, as he makes it less mechanical and more emotionally expressive.

There are still many tribes of American Indians who produce an essentially vocal music: the Hopis and Navajos, the Huicholes, the Lacandones, the Pueblos, etc. These last in particular sing without literary text. It is music extraordinarily expressive and very rich in nuances, called forth by the most legitimate human feelings, expressed exclusively with musical sounds whose intonation and intensity are varied interminably. Civilized occidentals generally call this music savage. It seems to me, however, to be among the most refined music I know. Its sincerity can only with difficulty be matched in occidental music. When I listen to this music, I think that it must resemble very closely that which man sang before fully developing his oral discourse, his language proper.

Music has been man's natural response both to the most elemental and the most complex necessities of expression. The most elemental—let us say the primary ones, produced by fear, horror, satisfaction, discontent, aggression, and sex—find a more direct and convincing medium than words in musical modulations of the voice. The most complicated and refined feelings likewise prefer the musical manner of expression, now that words and the oral phrase are too circumscribed by conventional significances, too limited by their precision of meaning.

The natural instruments for both music and language were the vocal organs. This first great stage, of music's dependence on the vocal organs, must have endured many centuries. First without words, then using them possibly in the manner of magic formulae, man produced the first music, his individual and collective songs. In almost all texts on the history and composition of music, we read that polyphony is a phenomenon not more than ten or fifteen centuries old. This asseveration is moving for the ingenuousness with which it is made. I return again to recall the indigenous psalmodies already cited, to assure myself that the music of the contemporary primitives is, par excellence, polyphonic. Few times can there be encountered clearer and more certain the recognition of the fundamental musical relations—the octave, fifth, and fourth—than in the primitive's intuitive discovery of them, long before any scientific speculation dwelt on them to found by reason any system whatever of scales and harmony. This consideration is important to us because it shows that the need for expression through music was so strong in the primitive that it drove him to discover complicated polyphonic and modulating forms. I cannot, of course, discuss here all the special considerations permitting comparison of prehistoric and contemporary primitives.

However, the satisfaction which song gave to the need for human expression could not be definitive or exclusive. Very soon man discovers the expressive power of the sound produced outside his body, by the vibration of wood, air, membranes, and little by little he begins to develop instruments to produce musical sounds. During who knows how many centuries of painful evolution, man arrived at making and using musical instruments determining a new and particular kind of music. Although the musical instrument was constructed and incessantly improved in accord with the anatomic and physiologic conditions of man, the period of becoming accustomed to its use was necessarily long and difficult. Before instruments, all music was sung; when they appeared, man, the musician, a singer by atavism, must have felt the instrument more as an obstacle to inspiration than as a new resource of expression. This discomfort lasted until he developed the new instrumental aptitude (which naturally did not exclude the vocal ability evolved through many centuries) from which instrumental music was born, its characteristics conditioned by that aptitude and by the physical possibilities of the instrument.

We see that the production of music consequently became substantially different the moment the instrument appeared. That is, given a need for expression, a determined feeling, and the same man would produce one given music if the expression were vocal, and another, with diverse characteristics, if it were instrumental. It is only necessary to realize this simple truth to understand to what a degree musical creation, music as a form of aesthetic expression, has depended on the physical condition of musical instruments. Further, the instruments have always been the product of the physico-mechanical advance of man. That is, a syrinx gives man definite resources of musical production, and that instrument could exist in relation to man's ability to whittle and bind reeds with the assistance of the mechanical instruments of the time. There could not have been a modulating, polytonal music (in the modern sense) even though in those remote times of the syrinx there had existed very strong musical individuals of great creative genius—for the simple reason that in that epoch there were no means of constructing pianos, organs, saxophones, violins, etc. In each epoch, the particular condition of art depends directly and exclusively on the degree of interior development of the individual, and that of the development of physico-mechanical resources he has been able to produce. Thus we can say that the production of music obeys the imperative need of human beings for expression, and the consequent capacity to satisfy it, but that the form and nature of its production are conditioned by the physical agent (instrument) which effectively produces the sound.

Musical Reproduction

Music is a fleeting process, with beginning and end in time. A plastic work, a painting or sculpture, is produced by its author on a permanent material. When the sculptor or painter has completed its production, the work remains thus forever. The musician, on the other hand, creates the music, which then has only the life lent to it by performance. This condition of music as an art *in time* (as opposed to the plastic arts, which have been called arts *in space*) has determined a practical necessity: that of reproducing more than once the music produced once. Furthermore, the practice of music has always been a phenomenon necessary not only to the individual, but also to society, and this fact confirms the necessity of reproducing the musical creation and performance of an individual for the good of the others. That is to say, for this reason, the reproduction of music is a social necessity—is, precisely, the means making possible the distribution and circulation of musical creation.

Music, like language, like other media mimic and plastic in expression, was growing in social value in proportion to the increasingly strong cohesion of the collectivity. From the moment when man's gregarious instinct begins to be felt, the means of expression—art, language, etc.—no longer seem to be the response to the need for expression which each individual must satisfy, but the direct answer to the social necessity for communication between the individual and his kind. When a human collectivity consolidates itself through community of beliefs, interests, etc., art and language must appear as means of satisfying a social need. With regard to music, there also appears at that moment the necessity to reproduce for the benefit of the collectivity the music which an individual alone has produced, obedient to his own need for expression and his natural creative impulse.

It is easy to discover the effective necessity for the reproduction of music, beginning in those primitive communes in which magic was a social practice of the first importance. Magic was exercised by means of figures, amulets, attitudes and special actions, but first and fundamentally by song. The power of expression in song, and the intense emotion it awakened in man's spirit, made him concede it marvelous power. Magic, the power of influencing invisible spirits, obeyed the formulae of imitation and repetition. The magic song was already music in our sense: a series of musical sounds subject to the phenomenon of rhythm (repetition) and acquiring a given form (imitation). There were priest-singers. There were special songs—to cure, to bring rain, to awaken or restrain the feelings of their fellows. These songs formed a reserve, a wealth of ritual value for the collectivity, the musical form of which had to be kept intact. The magicians transmitted their songs to the new priests; the people heard and repeated the music from generation to generation. It was the human memory, then, that was charged with perpetuating, reproducing, the traditional music.

As the forms of society evolved, music became associated with religious practices properly speaking, and with literary expressions. Finally, with the vocal and instrumental development of Greece, it came to have an expressive value independent of religious practices and literature, and was the object of special studies. We know that among the Greeks music was studied for itself, and that systems of sound were evolved conforming to scientific theories. To satisfy those necessities, it was not possible to transmit music from generation to generation exclusively by memory, which deforms and forgets. Furthermore, even in that epoch, the man of music had come to be conscious of his individual creations. He had the clear consciousness of being *author*, and the profession of artist-musician existed. The author could not submit to allowing *his* work to be deformed or lost, and, furthermore, he wanted it to take its place before others, to circulate. All this could happen only through a musical writing containing the music just as phonetic script contained the language. Then others would be able to reproduce the music which an individual had created, reading it, and he would not have to be the only performer of what he had composed.

The Greeks developed musical writing up to a

certain point, from where, after the founding of the Christian Church, it slowly evolved through the centuries. For a long time, music was reproduced, repeated in accord with a writing which still left much to the memory of the musicians. As a matter of fact, musical writing in its infancy was nothing more than a help to memory. But the theorization in which the Church was so rich during the Middle Ages allowed the formation, little by little, of a caste of professional musicians. In time, there came from it individuals of exceptional culture, peculiarly apt in music, individuals who would necessarily produce musical works conforming to their personal makeups, even though they were dedicated to, and nurtured by, the practice of a music as essentially collectivistic as religious music was. Then there arose a categorical necessity to be able to reproduce as faithfully as possible the music produced by a certain man.

Our present musical notation is a conquest made by long and patient effort. It began with little steps, small discoveries which collected, not with the precise and determined aim of arriving at a satisfactory writing, but as the sum of small accidents. Later, the musical works were the fruits of individuals whose imaginations were highly cultivated by specialization, and of the advances and complications of technique resulting from constant theorizing. These works, precisely because they were "advanced," required for their performance careful and repeated rehearsal, and also a more complex education on the part of the performers. It was then that theorists consciously began trying to develop a writing making the musical content more precise, minimizing the margin of error in order to facilitate performances by instrumental and vocal groups.

Paralleling the technical development of composition and notation, there was one of instruments. There was a constantly increasing realization that music is influenced by many factors of varying importance: the number, class, and quality of instruments; the merits of leaders; wise, inspired, or mediocre composers. Music was beginning to require specialized work. The seventeenth and eighteenth centuries knew that the pivot of the practice of music was notation, that without it, music—a fleeting process, a flash with beginning and end in time—could not be reproduced in different places at varying times.

Present-day occidental musical notation is far from supplying a completely satisfactory way of fixing musical concepts exactly and permanently. The margin of error it allows is very large, and it is suited only to the system of twelve tempered sounds. Even discounting these manifest limitations—which are more of the musical system than of its notation—the indications of the proportions of sonorities, of fine shadings of intensity or tempo, and many other fundamental factors, are highly approximate. There is no way of determining by means of an absolute value what the unit of sound-volume is to which the others can be referred in known and fixed proportion. Similar deficiencies occur in other systems of musical notation which have been proposed in the Occident— and perhaps even greater ones in those of oriental cultures, which in many instances are nothing more than procedures for assisting musical memory.

It would probably not be wrong to say that occidental musical writing in reality lacks the possibility of future development. The staff, the black and white notes, the clefs, the sharps, flats, and naturals, the dozen or twenty Italian words, and the not very great finality which the metronome can give tempi—these components of European musical notation do not give the impression of being able to develop into a really satisfactory means for precisely writing musical conceptions. We will do better to think that this means of permanently recording them will be found along new roads, just as music itself, in its natural and implacable development, will follow new roads.

Musical notation has had a fundamental value for the music it has served. Its greatest advantages could not be other than those of the music in which it is implied, and in which it came into being and developed to its present state. Later I shall speak of the importance which the act of definitively and permanently recording musical conceptions could have. At this point I want merely to refer to notation and musical memory as agents in the distribution of artistic production.

Whatever the conditions of reproduction may be, let us observe that what is important is that the reproduction of music is necessary and desirable because the phenomenon of production—creation—is rare and difficult to come by. The primitive magician-priest with his incantations, the composer of contrapuntal music, in fact any creator of music, requires the reproduction of determined works: the best of their kind. There has always been some music which is good, some which is bad. Good music is rare, difficult to produce, and therefore acquires a singular value. Its creator and the public repeat it.

If man's capacity for creating music were unlimited, the need to reproduce it would not exist. That need is in inverse ratio to the creative capacity. In other words, there will be greater necessity for reproducing music the smaller becomes the capacity to produce what is needed. The ritual singer produced dozens of songs to invoke rain, and both he and the tribe-members found one among them which inspired greatest confidence in the rite, which stimulated more, which evoked stronger emotion. On the next occasion, the same men would not sing the same song if they were able easily to produce completely new ones with expressive virtues greater than those of the song of the former occasion. The same would be true of the cithern-player, the troubadour, the singer of plainsong, and the modern instrumentalist. The limitation of the ability to produce music to a few individuals makes it inevitable that those who do create it cannot be the only ones to perform it. Their efforts would not be sufficient to satisfy the demand. That is why there are some who produce and others who reproduce. We see, then, that reproduction arises from very complex and varied needs. It is natural that in the general development of music men have constantly searched for and found always better means of giving stable existence to their musical creations: first memory, then notation.

Let us notice, finally, that such means were at first enough to make musical creation durable. Men sang, and engraved their songs on their own memories and those of others, from generation to generation. In subsequent epochs, similarly, musicians first created, and then attempted to make their creations permanent, using a constantly less defective notation. But the great growth of vocal and instrumental music and the consequent improvement in musical notation in our epoch have changed the order of these processes. Now the writing of music comes first, the performance later. Now, because of its complexness, the music of great vocal and instrumental ensembles can be created only as a reality of the imagination, and can come from the imagination only in the form of notation, not as performance. We cannot believe it humanly possible that the instrumental music of Wagner, Schönberg, or Stravinsky could have been performed before it was written. In order to *be*, really to come to life, this music with all its complexities requires an effective means of reproducing it. We see, then, that notation as a means of reproducing musical creation has come, because of its improvement and relative perfection, to be a decisive factor determining musical creation itself. Notation, born and perfected as a way of making musical reproduction possible, has been converted into a means for production also, for the creation of music.

The new electric apparatus of music production were conceived and developed by the physico-mechanical sciences as ways of repeating or reproducing the music of today. If they are satisfactory for that purpose, they are immensely more important as apparatus for the creation of a new and unthought-of music.

4. Electric Instruments of Musical Reproduction

BECAUSE of the enormous activity in the physico-mechanical sciences during the last decades, the twentieth century has seen the achievement of a high degree of development in various mechanical instruments of musical reproduction. These can be divided into two large groups: the first, made up of instruments originally played by men with their hands, arms, fingers, feet, mouth, etc., and the second, those instruments which, though not properly speaking musical, capture the vibrations coming from any sound-agent, using very divergent and complicated means to the end that they can reproduce the sounds identically, or almost identically, as often as desired.

First Group

Among the most important and representative instruments in the first group are the carillon, the orchestrion, the pianola, the piano-pianola or player-

41

piano, the electric reproducing piano (Welte-Mignon, Aeolian, etc.), and the reproducing organ.

Chimes originated in remote antiquity, and may be said to be a descendant of the Chinese *King.* Improved, they played an important role in the Middle Ages, both as a musical instrument in common use, and in the bell-towers of churches and other public buildings. The carillon, formed at first of four bells (*quadrilionem,* whence its name), had, by the twelfth century, been doubled or tripled in size. Its function is well known. Given its utility and importance in the life of medieval cities, there is nothing surprising in its large dimensions and elaborate construction. It was at first sounded by one or two men striking each bell directly with a hammer. When it developed considerably—as did the type of music played on it—a keyboard and pedals were adapted to it, making possible individual performances, and facilitating the emission of several sounds at once.

The direct antecedents of the carillon were the bells for marking the hours used before the invention of timepieces. The first mechanical devices for marking the hours and quarters come from the thirteenth century, before the invention of clock-faces. The first mechanism for sounding carillons properly speaking appeared in the weight-clock, in the fourteenth century. This primitive mechanism consisted of a wooden cylinder with spikes. The spikes, in turning, lowered levers which, in turn, moved mallets which struck bells. Thus, we may place the first mechanical apparatus of musical reproduction about six centuries before our time.

Little need be said of the cylinder-organ or the orchestrion. The former (called the *organillo.* in Spain, the *cilindro* in Mexico, the hand-organ in the United States, and the *orgue de barbarie* in France) may have originated at the beginning of the eighteenth century, and was, like the weight-clock, a barrel with pins. It was widely used in churches and residences, finally becoming, at the beginning of the nineteenth century, the small portable instrument so popular in the street. The orchestrion, a combination of piano and organ, was originally constructed, at about the end of the eighteenth century, as an instrument of direct performance. About the middle of the nineteenth century, it was converted into a mechanical reproducing instrument of considerable proportions.

In this group we finally come to the piano. Many systems of playing the piano mechanically were conceived in France, England, and the United States. It was in the United States, toward the end of the nineteenth century, that there was patented for the first time the mechanical piano operated pneumatically by means of a roll of perforated paper, the instrument known as the pianola or player-piano. The importance of this was enormous, though it was in reality only the last of the small steps taken during six centuries from the first mechanical carillon. The vogue of this instrument need not be described. Its efficiency in automatically and repeatedly reproducing piano music quickly made it a very important instrument for spreading music during the first decades of this century.

Throughout the course of its hectic development, the player-piano needed one very important improvement. It had to have the possibility of fixing not only the rhythmic, melodic, and harmonic character, but even the most delicate nuances of intensity and movement. This was finally achieved by constructive engineers, who took advantage of the great developments in electromechanics which have been taking place during this century. This important step led to the electric reproducing piano, which eliminated all direct human action (even the non-musical effort required at a player-piano) and by the fine exactness of its electromechanical apparatus made possible the identical unlimited reproduction of an artist's interpretations with amazing fidelity and precision.

It should be noted that electricity was the agent which, after the long development of reproducing instruments, made possible a completely new stage of evolution, in which the results obtained can be the means to a new level of perfection. Although electricity played no role in the inception of these instruments, or in their first improvements, it was required to cause a development of fundamental advance in their evolution.

The mechanism of the electric reproducing piano (Welte-Mignon, Aeolian, etc.) was also quickly applied to the pipe organ. Furthermore, even though no equally satisfactory applications of it to other instruments have yet been made, there is no indication that they will not, at a given moment, succeed.

The above sums up in a few words the process of the development of the first group of mechanical instruments of musical reproduction. It is important to note the purpose for which these apparatus were originated and developed. Thinking about this, we find that, in the case of the large or small carillon of the medieval bell-ringer, as well as in the big electric reproducing piano, the genius of man was applied to finding a way of replacing the direct human performance on an instrument with an equivalent mechanical one. The aim was to obtain greater ease, or greater facility of execution, which can easily be understood if we consider the fatiguing task of playing a piece of music on a bell-tower carillon each quarter of an hour of each day and night, year in and year out. Another aim, which was without doubt very important, was that of spreading music without the necessity of wide specialization in it as a profession, or of depending on performers not always at hand, or requiring a remuneration or compensation for their professional services. That is, it was appreciated that the mechanical apparatus would facilitate the spreading of music, not to the exclusion of the professional performer, but adding its action to his. This is what we can conclude when we consider the relatively great vogue of automatic pipe organs in the homes of French and English men of wealth from the end of the eighteenth century—and even more when we consider the vogue of the street hand-organ or the sudden great vogue of the player-piano. We could find other reasons explaining more abundantly the factors which stimulated the invention and development of these reproducing apparatus, but those already mentioned will suffice to give an idea of the legitimacy of the effort.

As to the artistic quality of the reproduction, we do not have many concrete data on the satisfaction our predecessors felt upon hearing the results of their inventions and the artistic quality of the reproduction. But, without a doubt, a continuing dissatisfaction must have been the incentive for new experiments. Judging by the results now at hand, we can say in this respect that these apparatus of musical reproduction (the electric reproducing piano in particular) well satisfy the exigencies of good reproduction.

However, if we go deeper into examination of the meaning of the development of these instruments, we find an observation to be made. Men sought a way of substituting for direct human performance of musical instruments an equivalent mechanical means—but they never considered or intended that the mechanism should do something different from, or better than, what they themselves did. It was not considered— and, it seems to me, is not considered now—that the machine, operating on the same principles which enable it to duplicate man's work, would also be able to do things outside his anatomic and physiologic limitations.

No attempt was made to create mechanical instruments which were not pianos, organs, or—recently— violins, the same instruments that had been invented and improved in accord with possibilities of human execution. Consequently, it was never considered that these instruments might do something besides repeat as faithfully as possible, and under the best conditions, the music created by men in accord with their anatomic and physiologic capacities.

Music Played by Mechanical Means

A pianola or electric piano plays mechanically a piece written to be played by the ten fingers of two hands, or by four hands. In this way, the instruments using perforated rolls have, and will increasingly have, validity as mere reproducers. But what in real-

ity the perforated roll offers us of greatest interest is
the possibility of a music not limited by the anatomic
capacity of two or four however dextrous and perfect
hands. Seen thus, the mechanical reproducing apparatus cease to have importance only as reproducers,
and become new musical instruments offering the composer unlimited resources. These, when fully exploited, will produce a new development in musical
literature. A roll can be perforated so as to obtain
simple and simultaneous rhythms impracticable for
the hands. On it there can be grouped sounds in harmony, and conjunctions of harmonies, impossible to
the hands. On it, finally, can be obtained successions
of sounds which, in their rapidity, or the distances of
intervals, would be absurd if judged by the present
concept of pianistic technique. Furthermore, by means
of the roll and the precision obtainable by complete
electric operation, there can be achieved perfect control of the intensity of sound, in the shading of fortes
and pianos in different voices or parts.

Pipe organs and violins are also operated by rolls,
and any other instrument could be played that way.
But not only the known instruments could thus be
played. There can be developed new types of musical
instruments, and of sound-agents in general, out of
sight of the human possibility of playing them directly with ten fingers, two arms, two lungs, two lips,
freed completely of those factors, and without any

limitation except the capacities of our ears, nerves, and intellects.

This electromechanical way of playing instruments not only makes it possible to obtain from each a rendition now unthinkable, but also makes possible the most perfect co-ordination of any number of them. It is easy to imagine the prodigies of polyphony and polyrhythm, of contrasts and amalgamations of sounds, which can be obtained by a large automatic electric symphony orchestra playing a music which only a roll, and no man or group of men, could possibly play. A composer taking advantage of all these resources to give form to his conceptions will be creating a new art, one still unforecast.

It will be thought that a musical coupling of this sort, so perfect a mechanical means of sound-production, will come to bankrupt the human feeling which is the only reason for the creation of music, and which the artists of all times have had to express through the language of art. But a belief of this sort would only reveal a complete lack of knowledge of the relation between man and the mechanical instruments he creates and develops. I have already spoken of the discomfort man feels with the instruments he invents and perfects, as long as he does not himself develop a parallel instrumental aptitude permitting him easily to take advantage of the new facilities provided by the instruments. Once this aptitude is achieved, however, he finds his capacity enlarged exactly in proportion to the efficiency and perfection of the instrument and his ability to use it. This truth is easy to understand. Once understood, it convinces us that man is fatally caught in an inevitable chain of progress. He develops always more nearly perfect instruments; that development, far from relieving him from developing his own capacity, obliges him to do so, for the new machine is otherwise without value. That is, it is man who commands, acts, thinks, and feels, and the machine has no other reason or significance than that of increasing the efficiency of his power, action, thought, and feeling.

The limitations of this book prevent me from going into fuller consideration of the controversial question of the relation between man and the machine. I want only to note in passing that the cause of the widespread mistake of believing that the machine, far from augmenting man's resources, limits him, is the disorientation produced in many people by misunderstanding and lack of knowledge of the innumerable deficiencies in our social organization. This same confusion would be felt by a Greek *aulos*-player, were he to find a modern oboe in his hands, or were he to find himself seated at the console of an organ with five keyboards, a system of pedals, dozens of registers and mixtures, all to be played by himself alone, using the extremely complicated electromechanical system of the modern organ—thousands and thousands of sound-tubes resembling the pipes which, twenty-five centuries ago, he played so successfully in Delphi, using the strength of his own lungs, the tips of his fingers, and one sound-tube, his pipe.

Not to expand this point farther, I believe it easy to conclude that the problem of every great instrumental advance is really the problem of discovering new human aptitudes related to the new instruments. That is, in reality, the heart of the matter. Up to now, the facts prove that man has been able not only to invent and constantly improve his instruments and machines, but also to develop exactly the capacity in instrumental aptitude I have been mentioning.

It is necessary, however, to make a distinction between man's role in relation to the musical machine when he is the executant and when he is the composer. We see that the possibility of playing contemporary or future musical instruments by mechanical means, when achieved, will allow freer and more nearly perfect performances. Equally, an ensemble of them becomes possible, as numerous as desired and controlled perfectly. This great mechanical symphony orchestra will have passed beyond human limitations of direct performance. It will, that is, have eliminated the human performer. At the same time, man has already realized and made possible new ways of intervening in mechanical operation. This means that the composer will have immensely greater resources at hand. His own musical creation will lead him to synthesize all the new possibilities and take into account the attributes of rhythm, harmony, timbre, etc., of the new instrumental form conceived. He will be obliged to multiply and develop to an extraordinary extent his aptitudes and capabilities. He himself will have to develop the new instrumental aptitude related to the complex new musical instrumentality.

It is sad that, for the moment, automatic electric instruments are static. Their rapid advance during the first two or three decades of this century was interrupted by the sudden appearance of other musical practices. I think that new attention should be given to the electric operation of instruments (whether by roll or some new system) when the advantages they offer are appreciated, and when electric instruments for producing sound—of which I shall speak later— have advanced farther. In view of the possibilities offered in its present state by electric performance by roll, and taking into consideration that, even though its development is spasmodic, there is no reason to believe that it has come to an end, it is possible to discover other important advantages of mechanical performance. Mechanical musical instruments of any kind—whether for reproducing music written for human performance, or for playing music written in view of the possibilities of mechanical execution (that is, unplayable by man)—eliminate the personal factor of the so-called *interpretation* by the human performer.

Performance and Interpretation

It is not only that every performer interprets according to his own feeling, but that it is impossible for him not to do so. The composer creates his music, and writes it so that it can be repeated. Musical notation proceeds by means of signs which do not fix with complete precision the musical values, tempi, shades of intensity and tone, balance of sonorities on the various musical planes, etc. It is clear, then, that there exists no physical medium allowing a performer to reproduce this writing without varying the music as conceived and written by its author. But let us suppose for a moment that musical notation is perfect, that it is a medium for fixing exactly the musical values of the original composition. This writing, even thus conceived, must be read by a man. Even though the shadings of intensity were expressed in decibels, the agogic shadings in micrometronomic units, and the pitches in exact numbers of cycles per second, man does not have in his organism means of responding with equal precision to such indications. Furthermore —and this is the most important thing—man, by reason of his moral and nervous makeup, has fatally to impress the style, character, and criteria of his own particular nature on everything he does. To think that a man, even obeying precise signs, can evade or contain the impulses of his own personality, eliminating interpretation completely, would be a fancy not to be considered seriously if it had not been insisted upon.

What are the reasons for this insistence? In the first place, without doubt, they are the unnecessary excesses of interpretation of many "prima donnas"—sufficient to cause irritation on the part of the composer and all sensible men. There is also a sort of repugnance or fear, always latent in a composer, of the possible excesses or deficiencies of interpretation to which his written musical work is subject. It is also possible to verify a historical tendency toward giving a musical work an unalterable value which will allow it to be compared with plastic works in respect to its complete integrity. If the interpreter alters the time, shadings, melodic character, balance of sonorities, etc., to the slightest degree, we are no longer listening to the composer's thought in its original integrity. This can please or disgust us—which does not alter the fact. Nobody can tenably hold that he has heard Beethoven's Ninth Symphony as Beethoven conceived it. Beethoven himself, on two consecutive occasions, may well have given two versions, two distinct interpretations of his own work. In contrast to this, once Michelangelo gave his Moses the last chisel-stroke, nobody, not Michelangelo himself, could make another version of the same work without detracting from the original. Each person can interpret the masterpiece of the sculptor for himself, but this interpretation has absolutely no effect on the sculpture itself. In the case of the music, the performer's interpretation directly affects the work itself.

In order that the desire faithfully to respect the original creation should have effective results, it must be expressed by means of indisputable practical validity. If the constant improvement in notation has been insufficient to preserve the musical work in its complete integrity, there is even less reason for those professions of faith which so many artists like to make—as, for example, when they declare themselves in possession of the "Beethoven Tradition," or when they make other more or less authoritarian declarations in regard to the passive role the performer *ought* to play. I have already pointed out that no material means exists to prevent anyone from interpreting according to his own feelings. Under present conditions, the goodness or faithfulness of an interpretation can never be determined with certainty. Nobody can definitely condemn or approve a performer's work with reference to the fidelity with which it reproduces the original thought and feeling of the composer. Those who nevertheless, in order to pronounce such judgments, pretend to an exact knowledge of the tradition of the classics, are merely using a mixed procedure, based partly on memory and partly on the writing. One such person, for example, pretends to own the Beethoven tradition because he once heard the Sonatas genially played by Liszt.

This really implies a backward step. This is to go back to relying on memory as the way to perpetuate or transmit a piece of music. Primitives relied on memory for their magic incantations. The first troubadours relied on memory for their love-songs. We know that this explains the successive deformations the music suffered. None of these earnest desires can lead to anything. They have no significance other than as symptoms of the tendency already referred to—that of giving the composer's conception an unalterable value. What it is most important to discuss at this point is the degree to which it is desirable to develop a reproducing means making possible unlimited identical performances of the composer's original conception.

Recalling the historical development of musical notation, we can make several important observations. First, notation evolved as a means of making the repeated performance of music possible. Music was constantly becoming more complex both harmonically and instrumentally, and memory was therefore becoming constantly more insufficient. Second, the perfecting of notation parallels this evolution of music toward constantly more complex forms. Third, by means of notation the value of an original creation is multiplied in various places and times, thus increasing the importance of its composer. Fourth, when music is transmitted by means of memory, the musician must have a personal aptitude similar, or very close, to that of the composer. Fifth, as the creation of music acquired greater importance, notation grew constantly more nearly perfect, and the role of the executant required less individual initiative.

The justice of these observations is evident even to those who have no special knowledge of the history of music. This is the general conclusion to be drawn: the historic evolution of musical notation indicates a tendency to make constantly more complex and important the phenomenon of creation or musical production, and to make the phenomenon of its performance or reproduction constantly more mechanical. That is, it indicates a tendency to make the musical work unalterable as originally conceived.

However, to complete the picture, we must still consider other facts which, while equally true, contradict the foregoing. First, when a performer pretends not to interpret, he lacks the emotion corresponding to that which produced the creation itself, and his reproduction therefore is neither faithful nor alive. Second, when he finds himself in an emotional state, he cannot help superimposing his personal expression on the composer's, even though within the closest parallelism humanly possible. Third, the public accepts a given performance as good and valid even though the interpreter alters and deforms the original thought, producing a new version of the original. This cannot be doubted in the case of popular musicians or in that of some eminent interpreters of classical music.

The general conclusion to be drawn from these observations is that a historical tendency exists which is completely contrary to the first one pointed out. Confronted by this contradiction, I take neither side, but simply conclude that, up to the present, the *modus vivendi* of music has been the result of the co-existence of these contradictory forces. Music was being conditioned by the circumstances in which it was born and has lived. While the production of music has involved the use of notation and interpretation, they in turn have influenced the nature of musical creation.

Let us, for example, look at the substantial difference between so-called folk music—not composed with any idea of being written down or preserved— and the music of cultured composers. The latter, in the first place, are strictly limited to the twelve tempered sounds, the only ones contemporary notation can record, while instrumental or vocal folk music always contains non-tempered pitches. The rhythmic complexion of folk music is often so complicated that its representation by our occidental system of measures would be extremely elaborate and difficult. The constant small irregularities in time and tempo in folk music cannot be captured in notation with complete fidelity. In addition, performance from this notation is very difficult for even the best professional performer, while for the folk musician his own music, however complicated it would be if written, is as easy and natural as any other act of his life. He sings and plays his complex music with the naturalness of a creator. Attempts to note this folk music down have never been satisfactory. It was not created to be written, or with the idea of making an unalterable image of it by any means whatever.

With regard to other music, it can be said with equal truth that it has been conceived with notation and interpreter in mind, and that without one of them its unity is destroyed. Experienced interpreters well know the high degree to which their personal initiative, emotion, and thought are required to give real life to the music lying inert on the paper. They know, too, what important results the smallest inflection or accent can have. Some contemporary masters, who

want a pure, non-interpreting performer, have undoubtedly never stopped to think what their art would
be if the director of the performance were not car-
ried along on the torrent of emotion their music
evokes. I have no desire to honor the virtuoso who
"makes use of music instead of letting it make use
of him," but I cannot believe that it is feasible to
serve music without animating it with the interpreter's
feeling. A manifest divergence between the composer's emotion and that of the interpreter is unac-
ceptable, but an absolute identity is inconceivable.
The problem, then, is not of using or being used by
the original conception, but of the composer and interpreter's agreeing with an inescapable minimum
margin of difference.

In order to answer the question proposed, then,
we must conclude that we cannot talk of an absolute
general necessity of fixing all music permanently.
One part follows a line of constant change. The other
part, on the contrary, evolves with a very marked
tendency to find constantly more precise media for
permanent fixation, for unlimited repetitions of performance identical with the original composition.

Mechanical Performance and Fixed Music

It is precisely within this last tendency that the
electric apparatus for musical reproduction represent

a possible practical and effective solution. It is foolish to desire man to become a mechanized performer who will not interpret, but will mechanically follow a non-existent perfect notation. It is far better to consider a humanized machine, one able to achieve, within its immensely more ample radius of action, an individual's fineness and high quality. Sound, by the very nature of its production, acquires from the human touch a living quality which no machine has yet equaled. Human touch is a decisive factor in sound-production on all existing instruments. On wind instruments it is the pressure of the lips on the mouthpiece, the special consistency of the tongue, the inflections of breath, the hands' support of the instrument in adjusting it against the lips. Each of these factors is a particular quality in each individual, and determines the beauty of sound according to the ability, experience, and musical feeling of each instrumentalist. On stringed instruments, as on the piano, it is the weight of the hand and arm, the elasticity of the muscles, the shape of the fingers, and many other individual attributes of each performer which determine the special color and quality of the sounds he produces. Up to the present day, this has been man's great privilege as against the machine in direct performance.

However, nothing indicates that electric mechanical instruments cannot eventually render the high qualities of touch which have heretofore been man's privilege. Against such an assumption must be placed the surprising perfection achieved by mechanical instruments (Welte-Mignon, Ampico, Aeolian, etc.) during the first decades of this century. The precision obtainable by electromechanical means is incomparably greater than that achieved by men.

Even in its present state, and accepting its limitations, the electric instrument is the only means now in sight for achieving music of fixed values unaltered during successive performances. When a mechanical performance outside current limitations has been achieved, the musical phenomenon which now includes creation and subsequent interpretations will be in the hands of the composer alone. He will decide everything—pitches, intensities, movements, rubatos, timbre, quality of sound—in short, the particular and related conditions of all the musical elements. Only then will a fixed music exist, and the musical creator, like the sculptor and painter, give actual permanence to his conceptions, beyond the possibility that time can alter or destroy them, or later extraneous intervention affect them. We can, and should, foresee the advent of this fixed music, basing our prevision on the historical tendency herein discussed— that of giving constantly better means and greater importance to the composer—as well as on the growing development of electromechanics.

We should not, because of this, desire the elimination of *music to be interpreted,* that is, the music which must be reanimated by human performance. On the contrary, musical thought is fluid by nature, subject to constant renewals and graftings. This is why, when we see a map of historic musical currents, we discover the most extraordinary mixtures, mutual influences between tendencies widely separated. The natural fluidity of musical thought and its constant integration and reintegration are not incompatible with the realization of a fixed music. That which will enable the perfect and permanent fixing of a musical concept need not impede many new versions of the same concept from being realized and equally fixed. Even less need it stop the sea of sane and noble musical thoughts humanity has produced and is producing from going on from person to person, sung or played as one of the most useful and valid means of binding men of different countries and epochs together.

With all these aspects in mind, we cannot do less than appreciate the great significance mechanical musical instruments have and will have in the history of music; the significance of electricity, which has been the element essential to their perfection. The physical means have developed so rapidly and fully that the musical development implicit in them has not been created simultaneously. Musicians do not yet have a clear notion of the relation between music and its physical agents—which is one more reason for writing this book.

Second Group

The second group of electric reproducing instruments includes, as stated at the beginning of this section, those not properly musical, which, by different means, capture the sound-vibrations coming from whatever sound-producing agent, and store them so that they can be reproduced identically as often as desired. They are the phonograph and sound photography. The fundamental characteristic of these apparatus is that they operate by a double process: recording of the sound and later reproduction of it.*

Beginnings and Development of the Phonograph

It appears that the Chinese, many thousands of years ago, were the first to try to preserve sound—

* Of great interest is the reference made by Dr. Alfred N. Goldsmith to another apparatus of this group. "There is another method of electrically recording and reproducing sound which is not so well known, but which has some possibilities. It is the telegraphone of V. Poulsen, invented almost a generation ago. It consists of a wire or band of a magnetic material (*e.g.*, steel) which moves through the field of stationary pole pieces of an electromagnet which carries the amplified microphone current. The moving wire is magnetized more

the human voice—by mechanical means. Little is
known of this scientifically, and the first accurate information we have of a practical result of this sort
of effort is that of the phonoautograph, with which
Leon Scott, in France in 1857, was able for the first
time to take down the track of sound by means of a
stylus on a disc of smoked paper, but from which
he could not obtain the reproduction. Twenty years
later, in 1877, Edison patented the recording phonograph and reproducer, after the most laborious investigations and thought. No desire to serve music
moved Edison to seek the solution of the problem of
recording and reproducing sound. On the contrary,
it is well known that he never thought of making
experiments with music until long after obtaining
satisfactory results, principally with the human voice.
That is, the inventor was not interested in music.
Even less did the musicians have anything to do with
the appearance and improvement of one of the most

or less in accordance with the wave-form of the original sound. If
such a wire is then passed between the pole pieces of a similar coil,
the magnetism of the moving band will induce voltages in this reproducer coil which can then be amplified and caused to actuate a
loudspeaker. The system is already used in England by the British
Broadcasting Corporation for the recording and subsequent reproduction of programs, and has recently found some applications in the
telephone field as well. Under more favorable conditions it is likely
to be further developed, and has the advantages that it provides a
practically instantaneous playback (without the usual processing of
disc records) and that records of great length (from several tens of
minutes to several hours) can be thus produced."

important factors for the evolution and development of music. This is worth noting, because it explains in large part the indifference and tardy reception which musicians offered this prodigious apparatus. We can all remember that so-called "serious" and cultivated musicians were completely indifferent to the arrival of the phonograph, and even, in many cases, refused it decidedly. It was only a short time ago, in our own time, that this situation changed. Two things with respect to this must still be hoped for: decided and systematic collaboration of musicians with acoustical engineers, and a clear vision of the immense new possibilities which electric recording-reproducing apparatus offer the art of music.

The chief essentials in the functioning of the mechanical phonograph are well known. The sound-vibrations, transmitted by the air and caught in a tube with a mouthpiece-like receiver, vibrate a diaphragm. This in turn transmits the vibrations to a cutting stylus which, resting on a moving wax disc, cuts a wavy groove whose form corresponds to the stylus' vibrating. The reproducing process is just the reverse, with the one difference that the stylus is replaced by a needle. In the apparatus the principal units are:

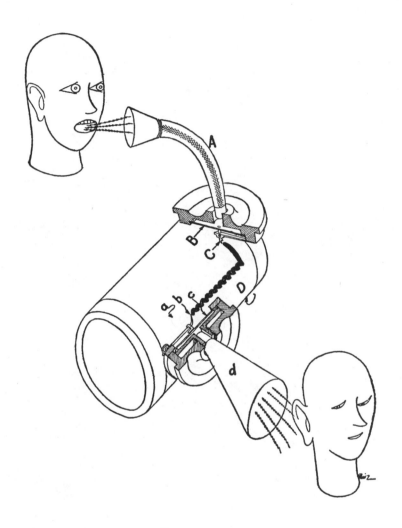

DRAWING 1

IN THE RECORDER:

A. tube with receiver
B. diaphragm
C. cutting stylus
D. wax cylinder

IN THE REPRODUCER:

a. wax
b. needle
c. diaphragm
d. speaker

The above-mentioned units are graphically represented on Drawing 1.

The general characteristics of the phonograph have not changed. Considerable advance was made by changing from the cylinder to the disc, and later in the better composition of the wax. But the phonograph made its first big step forward when advantage was taken for it of the most important discoveries of electroacoustics. Then the electric phonograph appeared. Its fundamental units are:

IN THE RECORDER:

A. microphone
B. amplifier
C. electric recorder
D. wax disc

IN THE REPRODUCER:

a. wax
b. electromagnetic reproducer
c. amplifier
d. loudspeaker

The above-mentioned essential parts of the electric phonograph appear on Drawing 2.

The microphone consists of a membrane (diaphragm) mounted so that the sound-vibrations transmitted by the air cause corresponding vibratory movements in it. These, in turn, produce variations in an electric current. These variations are amplified in a control panel by means of thermionic vacuum tubes. From them, the same current, thus modulated, moves the sapphire cutting stylus of the recorder so that the current's variations produce exactly corresponding variations in its movement. The stylus imprints on the wax a groove whose waves vary in accord with its movements. In the reproduction, the same phenomenon is reversed. As the needle runs over the disc, it undergoes displacements corresponding to the waves in the track. These displacements, or movements of the needle, produce corresponding variations in an electric current by means of an electromagnetic procedure. Amplified, these variations go to the electromagnetic loudspeaker. This is a cone of silk or other fiber in which a very fine wire

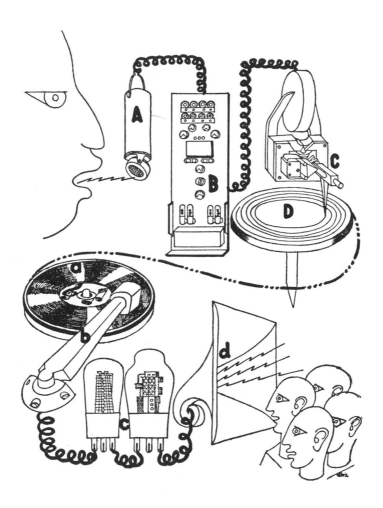

DRAWING 2

is wound so as to form a coil. The cone is mounted in a magnetic field. On passing through the coil, the current of amplified sound produces acoustic vibrations exactly equivalent to the vibration of the sound-agents which modulated the current.

The elements now used in the electric phonograph originated in various places. One year before Edison obtained the first satisfactory results from the mechanical phonograph—in 1876—Alexander Graham Bell had transmitted the human voice for the first time by means of electricity. This signified the birth of the electric microphone and receiver, and the other elements necessary for the electric transmission of sound. Bell's first interest was in the telephone, and had nothing to do with the phonograph discovered by Edison a year later, and even less to do with music. The telephone was limited to short distances for many years, and the phonograph stayed in its first phonetic stage, lacking electricity. There did not exist in electrodynamics any means of amplifying the tiny variations which the microphone produces in electric current. It was in 1907 that De Forest developed the thermionic lamp, initiated by the Englishman, John Ambrose Fleming, and by means of which the needed amplification could be achieved. A few years sufficed, once this fundamental element was perfected, for the telephone to increase its range suddenly, and for the phonograph to become electric.

The vacuum tube, as we commonly call the thermionic lamp, has been the *sine qua non* for long distance telephony, for the electric phonograph, the radio, and the sound film.

It has really been very fortunate for music that all these units—microphone, amplifier, loudspeaker, and the complementary equipment—have been developed outside the purely musical field, since in that strict field neither the necessary stimulus nor the indispensable economic resources have ever existed to bring to a head the laboratory work and gigantic investigations through which they have been obtained. It has really been in the laboratories of the American Telephone and Telegraph Company, and more recently in those of the Radio Corporation of America, that the chief advances in those branches of physics connected with the electric recording, transmission, and reproduction of sound have been achieved.

The reticence of professional musicians with respect to the musical importance of the phonograph is also due in good part to the ignorance of the constantly more rapid advance in the development of all the electric acoustical apparatus, and the consequent fear that the phonographic reproduction of sound will never be perfect. To realize clearly that the development of the phonograph is not only constant, but always more rapid, it is necessary to know the finest apparatus—which can be seen only in laboratories because commercial policy allows only a slow infiltration to the market of the finest models, in accord with a system which has nothing to do with the advancement of scientific investigation. To say that phonographic reproduction will very soon be satisfactory or perfect is not to make an arbitrary prophecy. It is to foresee the inescapable result of the present achievements of scientific investigation.

It is clear that to say "satisfactory" or "perfect" does not mean "impossible to better." Everything evolves constantly, and is always perfectible, both as to the thing itself and as to the standards of judgment of the people using it. The question is, then, whether it is possible to expect very soon the day when the most exigent demands of the musicians and public of today will be satisfactorily solved by the phonograph. The demands of the musicians will increase later—as will the proportionate advance of the phonographic mechanism.

The Electric Phonograph as a Reproducing Means

The phonograph, with all the improvements to which we have been referring, will solve two important problems: that of making music durable through satisfactory, identically repeated performances, and that of giving it wide and easy currency. Music is not always performed identically by human beings; each gives his own version; of these versions, many will be bad and many good; one of them will be preferable to the composer himself. It will be possible to preserve this one on a disc, allowing future performances always perfect and identical to each other. This will not prevent the making of new versions, adjusted more to the feeling of a certain interpreter or public than to the original idea of the composer. The rightness or wrongness of this is not the point in question.

There is a wealth of music spread throughout the world. Each country and region of Africa, Asia, Europe, America, has its particular music, which only with difficulty gets to other regions and countries. Furthermore, the constant process of the changing of the traditional music of all peoples brings with it the definite loss of this music in its first form. This is notoriously the case in Mexico. The traditional indigenous music is disappearing, and the present *mestizo* (Indian-European) music is evolving toward new forms of mixture. The record permits us to keep an exact image of the successive stages of traditional music. Thus, by means of the record, we can not only preserve the music of all countries, but also of all epochs. This great musical wealth ought to be spread from one country to another, it ought to bind humanity together. A great universal diffusion of music, realized in the double sense of geography and history, is a thing only the phonograph could achieve.

It is not to be doubted that perfect phonography will effectively supply an excellent means for the universal circulation of music—one we should desire and expect. Let us consider that the conditions for performing each particular kind of music are exclusive with an individual or determined group in each region. That is, it will be easy to practice symphonic music in New York or Paris (though even in these large cities there exist relatively few symphony orchestras), but it will be difficult or impracticable in thousands of small cities and towns of America and Europe. Equally, the music of the provinces is not easy of access for the big city. Music other than occidental is very defectively notated, and is given still more defectively in a performance from such notation. To all these problems, the record offers the only solution.

For several years, very considerable work has been done by some phonograph companies, artistic foundations, and European universities in recording exotic music. In the United States, some museums and institutes for investigation have been recording the music of the Indians on reservations. But even the great importance of these efforts is small in relation to the possibilities the disc offers for making perfect records of the musical wealth of the world. Many of these records are notoriously imperfect. Even when they exist, no satisfactory circulation of them has been provided, for this would require a special organization still to be formed. The libraries of records established in some universities, schools, and conservatories serve to spread music only in a very limited way.

Wired Transmission of Music

When speaking of electric phonography—and on Drawing 2—we indicated the fundamental units involved in the process. Let us cut out of this drawing the cutting on wax by means of the stylus, and the reproduction from the record by means of the needle. Our scheme would then be reduced to:

A. microphones
B. amplifier
C. loudspeaker

as can be seen graphically on Drawing 3.

Now we are not treating of storing music on a record for subsequent reproduction, but only of transmitting it by electric means in order to be able to control and dominate the sounds with all the resources of electric apparatus. Furthermore, we can by this means send music to great distances with ar-

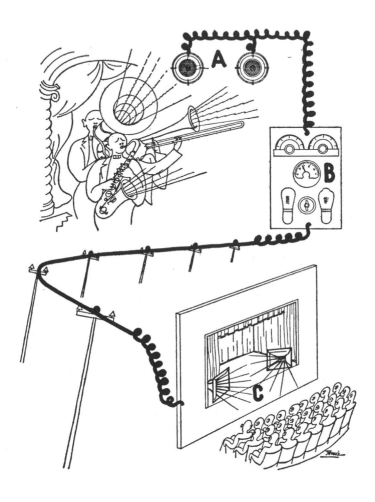

DRAWING 3

tistic results incomparably better than those achieved without wires by means of the radio. We shall consider the way in which this transmission can and should be performed.

An orchestra of traditional instruments plays music before one or several microphones; that is, the common orchestra is the sound-agent whose vibrations are going to be transmitted through the electric circuit indicated in Drawing 3. The microphone is an electric ear able to differentiate. We can have special microphones for high pitches of very rapid vibration, for medium pitches of less frequent vibration, and for deep pitches—and many more, for the differentiation may be infinite. As many microphones as judged necessary can be used in transmitting the music of a large ensemble. Each one of them takes in the sounds of special instruments, and sends them to their special amplification control, for the panel has an amplifier for each microphone being used. The output of all the amplifiers is mixed and sent to the final general amplifier, from which the modulated current goes to the speaker which converts it into acoustical energy. Thus we can use the control panel without limitation to make the most balanced compensations of sound-volumes. In this way a solo flute, for example, can be given all the volume desired, without forcing the reduction of the other sound-volumes. The disparity between the different registers of instruments can be obviated. Equal volumes for low and high pitches can easily be obtained. With such means of control, wired transmission can give to music a proportion in sonorities, a quality, and a general group of values which are impossible in direct audition.

The crescendi and diminuendi on a solo instrument or group of orchestral instruments are severely limited both in range and gradation; the electric amplifier has no limitation other than the human capacity to hear—the amplifications and reductions can be as gradual and regular as desired. It seems unnecessary to underscore the great significance which the easy and effective balancing of sound-intensities has for achieving the exact expression and feeling of musical speech. I shall nevertheless insist on one extremely important consequence of it when it deals with performances by groups of instruments each one of which has special conditions for the production of sound.

In the symphony orchestra, the necessity of balancing the most disparate sonorities establishes insuperable limitations. For example, a melody played in the low register of the flute has very little sound-intensity, and necessarily obliges the rest of the orchestra to play weakly. All the low registers of wind instruments are very somber, while their high registers are very brilliant and penetrating. This imposes serious limitations on the orchestration of passages in which both tessituras are needed at once. The bass violins and other deep instruments give a smaller volume of sound than the tenor, alto, or soprano instruments. In the present composition of the symphony orchestra, this results in a constant lack in the consistency of the basses.

Electric amplifiers make possible the solution of this general problem of compensating the disproportion of sonorities in an ensemble. One consequence of this is that for electric transmission the instrumental ensemble must be formed on a basically different criterion. In an orchestra heard directly, the quantity of the sounds is determined by the particular ability of each instrument to louden and soften, and by the grouping of equal instruments. We know that the capacity of each instrument is limited, it varies from instrument to instrument, and from register to register on the same instrument, and also with the technique of the instrumentalist. The variation in volume between the most attenuated piano and the most intense forte on a violin or flute is immensely more limited than the same instrument can achieve using an electric amplifier.

In ensembles, the addition of units increases the quantity of sound, but also changes its quality. By means of electric amplification, it is possible to take advantage of the quality of the solo instrument as well as instruments en masse, and in both cases to augment the quantity of sound without necessarily altering its quality. For example, electric transmission does not require the thirty-two violins used on concert platforms. In direct audition, for another example, it is possible to place a fortissimo trumpet solo against the fortissimo strings, but impossible thus to place a solo flute. By means of electric transmission, the two are equally practicable; a microphone adjusted to the flute will make it possible to hear it stand out from the ensemble as much as desired, by using its particular amplifier.

In an instrumental ensemble formed especially for electric transmission, we shall have to prefer the instruments which best preserve their timbre when transmitted, or those which better it. What happens to the timbre of each instrument when transmitted is now well known. It seems to me that the instruments which lose quality—for example, those of double reed and those with circular mouthpiece and mute—should not be eliminated, but should be studied with a view to using them and taking advantage of them with a realization of the deformations they suffer.

It can readily be understood, from the foregoing, that electric musical transmission radically alters the role of the conductor. He no longer fixes the balance of the orchestral sound solely in relation to the personal capacities of his players. Both before and during the performance he will regulate the amplification, using the control panel to obtain the musical result he wishes. Seeking a practical solution of this problem, it must be decided whether the director should be before his players or at the controls, or if it is possible for him to do both simultaneously. Up to now, a skilled and well-instructed operator has managed the controls satisfactorily.

The director continues to be confronted with musical problems, and those of his human instrumentalists. The work of musical interpretation, that is, of vivifying written music, is completed by the capacity or more or less profound genius of the conductor for solving musical problems in relation to human problems, and human problems in relation to musical ones. As long as music is performed by men, and orchestras are formed of instrumentalists, the most difficult problem in ensemble performance will be that resulting from the interdependence of the man and the music. The music depends on the man who is giving it life, and he in turn is undergoing in his psychological and intellectual being the direct influence of the very music he is playing.

It is evident that the more common the practice of transmitting music electrically—whether to record it on a disc or film, to broadcast it by radio, or simply to send it by wire to various places—becomes, the more pressing will become the necessity for directors to explore profoundly technical electric and acoustic problems, and for engineers to understand purely musical needs.

Leopold Stokowski has made very serious experiments with musical transmission by wire. He made one at short distance and one at long, the first within the Academy of Music in Philadelphia, and the second from Philadelphia to Washington, D. C. They consisted of transmitting the music from a closed room in the Academy—in which the orchestra was installed—to the stage where the loudspeakers were located. The placing of the microphones, the operations of mixing and amplification, the installation of the loudspeakers, all were carefully studied and tried out by the Bell Telephone engineers working with Stokowski.

The audiences at these concerts had a strange impression, seeing the stage vacant, completely unoccupied. They could see nothing in place of the orchestra, not even the loudspeakers, which were hidden. But their amazement was even greater when they began to hear the orchestra with the same perfection, the same life and quality, as though it were there before them. The success was extraordinary. Stokowski obtained unhoped-for musical results, in the balance of sound-volumes, in sound-modulation, in the effectiveness of the crescendi and diminuendi. The effect was that of sound extraordinarily well outlined, balanced, and accentuated. Some people object to such a presentation of music, it not being traditionally "proper."

These electric apparatus have been used only for transmitting classical music conceived within the limitations of direct human performance. When subjected to this "treatment" of highly efficient balancing by means of electric apparatus, this music undergoes a manifest alteration, if compared with the composer's original conceptions. The various reactions to this fact will not easily be reconciled, but they do not seem to me to be very important. What is needed is the new music conceived in terms of these new resources. Musicians are slow to understand the opportunities offered them by these new media. But this is true not only of musicians. When I discussed these questions with a friend of mine, he told me that architects are far from having created the architectonic conceptions which will take advantage of all the gigantic resources inherent in reinforced concrete. We must hope that these new conceptions will begin to take form when the young musicians of this generation understand the artistic significance of these new instrumental resources.

In what we have said about reproducing instruments substantial support can be found for the contention that musical thought is always relative to a reality of performance. Art expresses human thoughts, feelings, and emotions, and its expression will always achieve greater amplitude and clarity as the physical means of externalizing them become more capable and full. Each music is related to a particular instrument, and each instrument is related to a particular music. No music can exist which is not related to determined instruments and their possibilities, which necessarily have a physical limit. I should like to know whether the most mystically inclined man, in a divine and miraculous rapture, has ever heard "celestial music" that was not played on harps, flutes, and trumpets, or sung by voices—human voices—like those heard here on this earth, in our churches, theaters, and cabarets.

5. *The Sound Film*

~~~~~~

ALONGSIDE electric phonography, among the means of musical reproduction is the photography of sound, that is, a way of registering sound by means of a photographic impression. Sound-photography in itself has an enormous interest for composers, in that it offers new and very ample musical resources. But given the conditions in which it was born and lives, and its function in cinematography, I shall not be content with merely judging it as an independent musical medium, but shall try to consider all the musical aspects of sound photography in relation to cinematographic art as a whole.

The general procedures of sound cinematography and the essential points in the production of sound films are not very clear even in the minds of many people interested in the cinematographic art as such. For this reason, a brief glance at these matters is not without interest, and will give us the basis for later consideration of the capacity of these mechanical means of musical reproduction—developed in the last few years as a result of the tremendous general scientific advance—for the development of new forms of cinematographic musical art.

The Photography of Sound

The entire process of sound-photography embraces, as with the disc, the recording and reproduction of sounds. The apparatus for recording includes the following fundamental parts:

A. microphone
B. amplifier
C. light-valve, or oscillograph
D. sound-track on the cinematographic film

For the reproduction it includes:

a. exciting lamp
b. sound-track
c. photoelectric cell
d. amplifiers
e. loudspeaker

These parts are represented graphically on Drawings 4 and 5.

The vibrations started by the sound-agent, transmitted by the air, produce a corresponding vibration in the diaphragm of the microphone. These vibra-

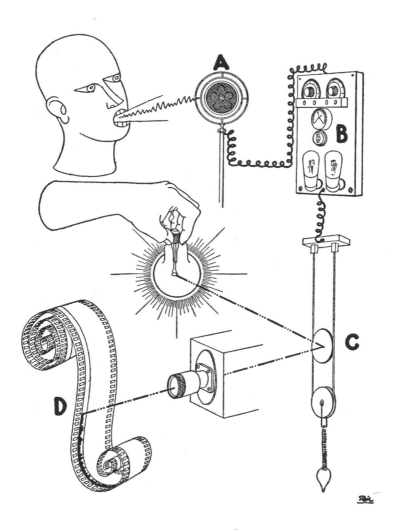

DRAWING 4

tions (or variations of pressure on the diaphragm) produce corresponding variations in an electric current which, connected with a lamp, cause variations of intensity of light corresponding to the variations in the current. The rays of the lamp are projected onto a cinematographic film passing by at a constant speed of ninety feet per minute. The variations in the intensity of the light produce a continuous impression on the film, the greater or lesser density of which corresponds to the greater or lesser amount of the light emitted by the lamp. This continuous impression, made on a narrow band along the side of the film, is called the variable density soundtrack.

In addition to the method described above, the Western Electric, there is also the R. C. A. Photophone system (of fixed density, or variable area) which uses a vibrator or oscillograph. This system consists of passing the current coming from the microphone through a Blondel oscillograph. The thin laminated wire of the oscillograph, provided with a tiny mirror, vibrates in accord with the variations of the current. The reflections of light from the mirror, in their turn, reproduce the movements of the oscillograph, and are impressed on a cinematographic film.

To obtain the reproduction, this film is passed through the projector in the usual way. A ray of light produced by a system of lights penetrates the sound-track, and passes to the photoelectric cell. The quantity of light which the film will allow to pass varies in relation to the variations in density of the photographic impression of the sound-track. The photoelectric cell can be easily understood as a simple resistance varying in direct relation to the quantity of light it receives. That is, composed in one of its essential parts of a photoactive metal, its conductivity of electric current is variable in proportion to the amount of light it receives. The photoelectric cell produces variations in an electric current, variations corresponding exactly to the variations in intensity of the light it receives. These variations depend on the density of the photographic impression, and correspond exactly to the variations in the current which produced them in the microphone when it was affected by the sound-agent. In this way, the electric current coming from the photoelectric cell, thus modulated and later amplified, places the diaphragm of the loudspeaker in vibration. It in turn produces acoustical energy exactly equivalent to that which originated the whole process.

The general outlines of sound-photography, seen thus in bird's-eye view, are astonishingly simple. Nevertheless, their detailed practical realization is highly complicated, and requires equally complicated instruments and machinery. The reader inter-

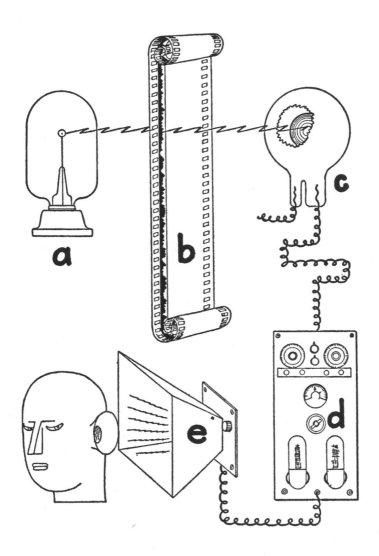

DRAWING 5

ested in these details should consult specialized works on the subject.

Apparatus of the Sound Film

The media used by the sound film are the photography of sound and phonographic reproduction synchronized with the projection of the visual image. The production of films has developed two procedures of filming: (1) the recording of the sound simultaneously with the taking of the scenes, and (2) the recording of the sound separately from the taking of the scenes.

By the first of these procedures, a simultaneous recording is made of the visual and aural parts of a scene or action. Innumerable difficulties had to be overcome to make this possible, as the hearing function of the microphone cannot be limited. It records everything it hears. Men both listen and hear—that is, we can hear a thousand sounds and listen to only one—but the microphone knows no such distinction. It listens to everything it hears. For this reason, a thousand limitations appeared in the first apparatus. Directors, accustomed to giving loud shouts to direct their actors, assistants, and operators, found themselves suddenly in the very annoying situation of either keeping absolutely quiet or having their cries and exclamations recorded faithfully on the film.

The cameras had to be turned silently or placed in soundproof containers. The general system of orders had to be silent also. Until special stages and all the necessary soundproof equipment were developed, there was the ridiculous situation that the traffic department of Hollywood had to stop the movement of vehicles for ten square blocks around a studio (many of them are located in the center of the city) when sound films were to be recorded.

Even that is not all. One of the fundamental difficulties in the simultaneous recording of sight and sound was the placing of the microphones on the stage, where they either interfered with the vision or were not acoustically well located. The truth is that, up to the present, this problem has not been solved satisfactorily. The separate recording of the sound, however, has come to have the necessary efficiency. Once the mechanical problems of synchronizing sight and sound had been solved, it was easy to solve that of joining sight and sound recorded on separate occasions. Synchronization is the solution of two purely mechanical fundamental problems—that of discovering the relative normal speed at which the apparatus of sight and sound should function; and that of discovering the manner of recording on the two apparatus at that uniform speed. Electrodynamics solves these problems without further difficulty.

The special details of the system of synchroniza-

tion need not be described here, though they are not
without interest. A well-established system of meas-
urements of time and length of film, fixed by means
of signs and special marks, has developed synchronization to a point where it is without danger or deficiency.

A world of new and unlimited artistic possibilities,
huge and almost virgin, is revealed to us when we
consider the musicalization of a film with all the resources of the laboratory. That is, we shall not be
content with the sound which the microphone can
capture during the taking of the scenes, however fine
the installation and condition of the stage. We shall
take the scene and the sound separately. We shall go
from the action-stage to the laboratory. We must
choose between making the sound-recording first and
the visual second—the procedure called pre-scoring
—and the reverse, or post-scoring.

In any case, the recording of the sights and sounds
should follow a single preconceived plan including
both: the complete plan of the film. The preconceived plan, though subject to more or less important changes (directors varying greatly in this respect), allows place for a special sound-script. All the
means at hand will be used for this montage: simultaneous taking of sight and sound, post-scoring, and
pre-scoring. Both plans—the general and the sound—
will be used later in the final montage of the work.

Sound-Material

Acoustics and acoustic architecture have had parallel developments to that of the electric transmission of sound. It is part of them. In a few years of extraordinarily intense cultivation, this science has obtained the fundamental knowledge necessary for determining what are the best conditions for recording-stages as well as what its own best procedures are. This is a science which the movie musician, without becoming a specialist, should know in its fundamental aspects if he is to know perfectly the requirements and conditions of the material he uses for creation: sound.

The finest recording installations are used. The music of orchestra, of song, of whatever type, played by the traditional musical ensembles and with the customary synchronizing procedures, is prepared and recorded. But there is another sound-medium which is not music, which we could call semi-musical: noise and other sounds which lend atmosphere. For these, use is made of an orchestra of instruments not truly musical. There are tremendous ensembles of instruments for producing noise or semi-musical sounds, collected with great patience and supreme ingenuity by the music departments and engineers of Hollywood. These are really worth seeing. In addition to all the known percussion instruments—which have undergone the most curious variations—and the collections of sirens, klaxons, and machines for imitating wind, thunder, rain, the roaring of the sea, raging mobs, etc., there are the most ingenious electric resonating instruments for producing the most unexpected noises and murmurs. It can be seen at a glance that the variety of instruments has been uncommonly increased to fill the needs presented by the sound film.

But there are even more. Sound-agents are not limited to the above-mentioned instruments. There are all kinds of sounds, of nature, industry, and city, specially recorded on the spot on a sound-track or disc, to be stored, and thus remain available for use at any given moment. There have thus been formed the so-called libraries of sound, in which thousands and thousands of noises, sounds, murmurings of nature and man in thousands of different places and times, have been preserved.

The music of the film, then, does not depend only on the normal resources, the thirty or forty sound-elements which compose the most complicated classic symphonic score. Here at hand, ready to be used in our creations, are all the sound-elements possible or imaginable. This wealth, this ensemble of controlled and manageable sound-elements, is a fabulous story difficult to believe. It is nevertheless a fact. The store

is there, and for everybody, for anyone wanting to
use it.

It will be some time before we can try to evaluate,
even in a general way, the musical possibilities of
the sound film. Let us now go ahead with our review
of the laboratory resources.

Re-recording

In the process of re-recording, we use a reproducing apparatus—either the sound-track or the disc
type—and we re-record the sound on a new sound-
track or disc. In the course of this re-recording, we
can use all the resources of electric transmission. We
can amplify all or parts of the sound, correct the
tempo, give accents, or weaken certain passages.

For example, we have a record of the noise of the
sea. The reproduction is faithful; the sounds of the
sea come from the disc just as they sounded when
recorded on the beach. Suppose, however, that we
need the sound of the sea in a gradual crescendo,
because, let us say, we are creating the effect of it
to someone approaching a beach gradually. After-
wards, the noise of the sea is to diminish suddenly,
because the attention of the listener is changing violently under another stimulus. We are to continue
hearing the sea, but weakly. Then the sound is to

surge back and the person to move slowly away from the shore.

To obtain this effect, we go through the operation of re-recording, during which the disc or track containing the natural sound of the sea is passed through a reproducing apparatus. This sound passes to an amplification panel, and from there is re-recorded on a new disc or track. At the beginning of this operation, we shall shut off the sound completely by means of the amplifier, gradually opening it slowly to obtain the effect of gradual approach. Later, we will diminish the intensity when the person's attention has been distracted, and still later will increase it suddenly and begin a gradual diminution as the person moves away from the shore. On the new disc or track we shall have the necessary modulations and gradations.

Re-recording is also used to correct defects in the first recording, resulting either from flaws in the original performance or from the mechanical process of recording. When an excess of sounds of high pitch is to be corrected, for example, special filters are used at the time of re-recording. Furthermore, re-recording makes possible the superimposition of as many sound-images as desired. The amount that can be done in this way is prodigious. Coming from the microphones or reproducing instruments, sounds, murmurs, and noises, in whatever quantity and intensity wanted, can be recorded simultaneously on the sound-track.

Drawing 6 shows the apparatus for a multiple re-recording, producing what is called in cinema jargon "mixing." On it can be seen:

A. microphones
B. reproducing apparatus of the sound-track
C. reproducing apparatus of the disc, sending its sounds to
D. the mixing panel

Here the various sonorities are mixed and, having been modulated, are sent to

E. the recording apparatus of the sound-track.

A mixing of, say, four, six, or eight sound-images is an action which, even when done by an engineer or operator, requires a well developed and defined musical sensitivity. It involves giving each sound-image its precisely correct proportion by means of the amplifiers and filters.

In the present stage of production, the superimposition of sound-images is constantly used: a dialogue, a subdued musical background, a general atmosphere, formed, let us say, of the confused noise of voices in a room, and finally the so-called incidental noises—the closing of a door, a shot, a telephone

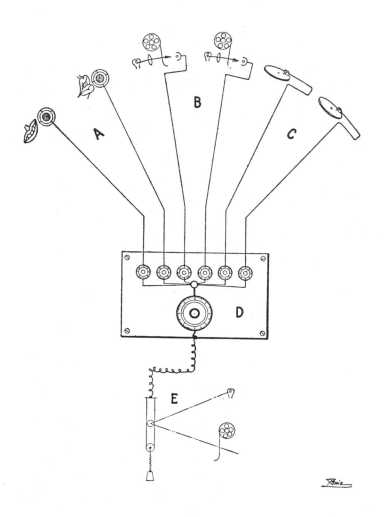

DRAWING 6

ringing, etc. All this sound-material should be measured and compensated with the same musical sense used by the director of a symphony orchestra in his task. The only difference is that the sound-material in this case is much more complex than even that supplied by the most complicated modern symphony orchestra. A glance at the practice of "dubbing" will further clear up this important point.

Dubbing

In movie slang, dubbing means the joining together of those practices and procedures of re-recording necessary for the montage of a film which are not precisely those related to the synchronous taking of sight and sound. Dubbing includes pre-scoring, post-scoring, and the various kinds of re-recording. Let us suppose a scene in which there are simultaneously (1) dialogue, (2) subdued musical background, (3) atmosphere (murmurs of talk and a storm outside), and (4) incidental noises, as shown on Drawing 7.

First, a sound-track will be made with the two elements necessary for the atmosphere. Then a multiple re-recording will unite the three tracks—dialogue, musical background, and atmosphere. During this process, it will be necessary to reduce the intensity of the music and amplify the dialogue, as well as give the atmosphere the alternations of intensity and speed required by the other elements. Then we shall have a single track containing the first three elements. Still later, the incidental noises must be added. For this, a new track will be made, on which the other track will be recorded at the same time that the incidental noises are made and recorded.

This short description of a conventional dubbing will serve to indicate in practical terms the sound film's extraordinary wealth of resources. Dubbing is, let us say, the procedure by which the movie musician integrates his orchestra of music, sound, words, and noises, the most complex orchestra man has thus far developed.

The Films and Contemporary Music

With this wealth of resources in mind, we might think that we should be witnessing the production of real musical masterpieces in the films, that we should be seeing the contemporary musicians turning their activity toward this fertile field. Neither of these things, however, is in sight. A few years ago, a noted French musician gave the signal-cry. Recently —also among the cultured musicians of France— serious attention has been paid the sound film, but with a pessimistic attitude. One, for example, laments that Ravel does not make films. Another laments the

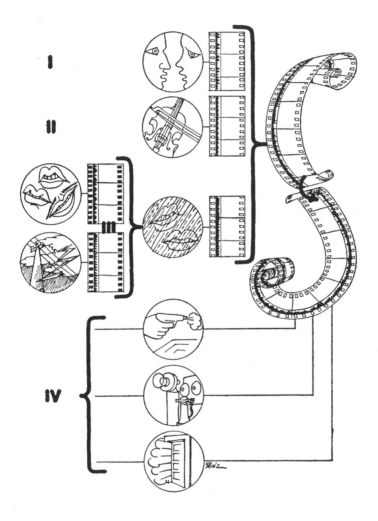

DRAWING 7

lack of an aesthetic of the cinema, and all denounce the producers.

There are no indications of essential changes in contemporary musical production resulting from the appearance of the sound film. Composers go on writing only classical symphonies, symphonic poems, string quartets, operas, masses, sonatas for piano and violin, etc., and the arrangers of the producing firms control the production of films. The former live comfortless, with sparse elements of life and action, agonizing to achieve a Paris or New York performance of their works, directed or interpreted by some celebrated artist. The arrangers live in ease. They arrange, compose, or prepare the music the public of the whole western world constantly hears in movie-theaters. This music has a constantly enlarging public, while so-called contemporary music is produced only with difficulty.

It would be easy to content ourselves with the answer that there will always be an elite music for the minorities and a popular music for the masses, and let it go at that. But this over-simple answer will suffice only with difficulty, for it requires us to believe that the most cultured and intelligent artists, the so-called geniuses of art, those who have created its progress, have always produced an art for minorities, and that the majorities have never been able to like and make use of lofty human conceptions. This we cannot believe, for the facts prove it false. The widely held belief that geniuses are misunderstood beings who exist on the edge of society is a vulgar mystification very easy to dispel.

The great Greek artists, those who produced the great flowering of music, poetry, and tragedy, were national heroes—during their lives, not later. They represented the taste, thoughts, and feelings of the whole people, who recognized them as their own. The music of the Roman Catholic Church was the music of everybody for fifteen centuries. The first great intellectualized individual creations (those of the polyphonists) were not works for minorities, but for everybody, with a value measuring up to the social needs of their epoch. It would not occur to anyone to think of Palestrina as a misunderstood genius. The same is true of Bach in the German Church. Up to the present, the Church has been the largest and most powerful institution cultivating and practicing music as part of its habitual functions. Nothing could have been more natural than that Palestrina or Bach should have created the music of their Churches. They became great in carrying out an effective social function. The Church always had in it all the great musicians, who were never far from the masses, since they absorbed by instinct and without effort the popular music in which their respective regions were rich.

After the Renaissance, when the Church was not the only force that counted socially, there was a theatrical-musical movement culminating in the opera. This was a true social institution, and its artists were also national heroes, during their lives, not later. A material proof of the social importance of opera is the simple observation of the form in which, during the eighteenth and nineteenth centuries, the opera-houses appeared. Each city built its theater, just as we build our cinemas today. Rameau, Lully, and Gluck in France; the interminable list of famous Italian composers culminating with Rossini, Verdi, and Puccini; Purcell and Händel in England; Spohr, Weber, and Wagner in Germany—all these were masters of a living art, untiring workers who produced their artistic works to satisfy an effective social demand. During their lives, they enjoyed the favor of the masses they served.

The fact that some of these men were hissed at first simply means that the constant natural advance of human thought is slower in the masses than in individual creators. The thirty years that intervened between the first time Wagner was hissed and the approbation the public gave him once they had recognized themselves in his works, do not disprove the social value of the works. There have always been difficult periods of transition, both for the public and for the artists, when the current forms of expression begin to crumble, and the new forms have not yet been consolidated. The present epoch is a typical case of this painful frustration: the opera and operetta have not finished dying, and the sound film has not finished being born. It is equally true that the cases of decadent art found in history correspond to stages of society which were decadent. But the fact that there are always decadent social strata does not mean that humanity is disintegrating, sociologically speaking.

Conditions and Criteria of Cinematographic Production

Cinematography as dramatic representation, and sound-cinematography as dramatic-musical representation, had from the beginning a success which need not be described. In this success, however, we should distinguish between that achieved by the pure novelty of the medium and that achieved little by little through the use made of these media for the creation of dramatic and dramatic-musical art forms. That is to say, at their inception the movies offered the public the attraction of pure novelty; people went by the thousands to see with great glee a man walking, a train moving, an unknown landscape, a sudden change of scene or panorama, or a cinematographic trick. This was the success obtained by the movies as a new and unexpected medium. Everyone, adults and children, went to those movies of the early years to see the greatest foolishness.

But very soon the public needed to find an interest in the content, and the movies thus began to be a form of artistic representation using the cinematographic medium. We do not have to understand by "artistic representation" more than the necessary formalization of a film in which there are developed a certain number of facts and images conforming to a preconceived plan or interweaving, and which tend to represent or synthesize human actions, situations, and characters of one kind or another. Now we see that in the cinematographic art, as in any other, diverse artistic conditions exist, depending on the degree of talent or genius of the creator.

Cinematography as artistic representation is distinguished from documental cinematography in that the latter registers human or natural phenomena as they are produced naturally. In this sense, a documental film presents the growth of vegetables, the propagation of microscopic larvae, the consummation of a crime taken on the spot, or the horrors of war taken at the front. The documental films also include the newsreels, which have been so successful with the public. This type of film is enormously important for a thousand reasons, and often has greater aesthetic value than the other type.

However, in this book I shall concentrate solely on the so-called artistic film, as it is on the sense of representation and the degree of expressive synthesis that the existence and condition of *cinematographic form* depend. Cinematographic form should fit the movies' resources, just as a musical form should fit orchestral resources, or architectural form constructive resources. We would laugh at the idea of a reinforced concrete bridge having the same form as one of the huge stonework bridges built by our ancestors.

It is undeniable that from its infancy movie production has been following this course. That is, it seeks a constantly more adequate relation between form and cinematographic resources. We all remember that movies in their earliest stages operated with the resources of the theater. Naturally it could not have been otherwise, the theatrical drama being the form of expression closest to giving it an antecedent. From then on, the movie forms have become constantly more cinematographic and less theatrical. But the appearance of sound as a new movie element has caused, on one hand, the transplantation of the operetta and review (musico-theatrical forms) to the screen, and on the other hand a simple superimposition of sound onto the dramatic form, sometimes with excess of realism or arbitrariness.

The truth is that during its silent period movie production advanced a great deal toward the achieve-

ment of a properly cinematographic form, while the
sound film now makes us feel, most of the time, that
its own resources are being used improperly. Now
we see that the solution does not lie in the filmed
operetta, even less in dialogued drama with "musical
illustrations" and "incidental noises," as now generally made. There must be another solution. The
form of the sound film must be a synthesis of all the
expressive resources inherent in the media. Drama,
the plastic elements, action, music, and literary content should form an organic whole. Greek tragedy
aspired to a similar unity. Wagner sought it in his
music-dramas.

This is not the place to discuss these forms or the
reasons why time has not respected their integrity.
The music and miming of the Greek theater have
not survived, and the music from Wagner's dramas
has attained a life separate from them. All I wish to
point out is the evidence that, for the achievement of
an artistic form synthesizing all the arts, we need a
material medium guaranteeing their proportional
development and making their union physically possible.

The sound film is undoubtedly this medium. But
it will be impossible to achieve this synthesis in the
direction in which, as a rule, the present standard
production goes. A novel, written with no cinematographic sense, is adapted by a scenario writer. The

director, limited by the financial policies of his firm, and by the inescapable necessity of enlarging the importance of the role of one or more stars, proceeds to the filming. The scenario writer and the director know little or nothing of the possibilities of musical expression. The music and sounds are added later by a "sound-expert" in collaboration with an arranger specializing in *pasticcio*.

But do not let us think that this situation is arbitrary or unchangeable. The appearance of the movies was so sudden, and their development so violent, that they had to use the first artists at hand. Those of the greatest aptitude and preparation did not enlist. Their identification with the theatrical, musical, or literary forms of the past did not permit them to turn suddenly to the new medium. It would have been impossible, in 1926 when the sound film first appeared, for the great and famous musicians suddenly to have dropped their symphonies, quartets, and operas, considering that they had been following those forms from their childhood. The same is true of the novelists and dramatists. On the other hand, as was the case on the first appearance of the silent films, the public is content, during the sensation of the novelty, with the purely sensual aspect of the product, and does not demand much from its contents or quality.

This is why, not counting on artistic collaborators

of good quality—for the reasons mentioned—and having to fill a demand both fabulous and unparticular as to quality, the standard production was the only solution. The production of the standardized film served marvelously the commercial interests of the movie firms, but this fact does not allow us to conclude that those interests are the only obstacle to the production of good films. The present movie industry has the best group of scientists available to solve all the industrial and physical problems. It does not have, in the field of artistic creation, a group of collaborators of the highest quality because, at present, those who by their personal aptitudes could be the most able have not realized all the immense possibilities of the sound film.

No musical creations taking advantage of the wealth of the film's sound resources have yet appeared. Up to the present day there have as a rule only been what might be called musical salads, concocted of the most vulgar and sentimental tunes and realistic sound-imitations, giving the ensemble a naturalistic character of the poorest sort. Music has not even played its expressive role in the balanced ensemble of the other cinema arts. The commercial firms producing films have no interest in improving the public's standards. This is an undeniable fact. But it is also a fact that, in the full bloom of capitalism, there have been produced, without economic limitations, films of as high artistic quality as their producers could develop. It is also a fact, finally, that if the commercial firms do not stimulate (or even if they lower) the quality of public demand, that demand is nevertheless fatally raising its own standards, because in the general course of sociological development constructive attempts and positive reactions must finally prevail.

The Church never lost money by procuring the highest artistic creations of a Palestrina or a Bach. The great theatrical impresarios of the eighteenth and nineteenth centuries, who were the focal points of the production and spreading of opera in Italy, Germany, France, and England, did a profitable business with the best artists, composers, and performers of the epoch. We must understand the historical reason for the standardized film, then, and not use it to foment a pessimistic attitude.

The fact that the movies are the medium of expression of our own epoch cannot be denied. As an organization for spreading ideas and feelings, their power is unequaled. In this sense, the movies are an institution comparable only to the Church in its best times. Each place, from the great city to the smallest hamlet, has its movie-theater. It is evident that neither the book nor the magazine, nor even the daily newspaper, penetrates the consciousness of humanity with the constancy or objective persuasiveness of the movies. Their social value will constantly be taken advantage of more directly in favor of the particular educational or political tendencies of governments. In Russia, this has been done openly. It is a fact—though not openly admitted—that in the United States the educational results of the movies serve this or that political interest.

After considering these factors, then, we must hope for the efforts needed to create a legitimate cinematographic form, a synthesis of all the concurring arts. We must also hope that it will serve a just and elevated social interest. There is no object in trying to formulate an aesthetic for the movies. To do this would be to substitute one routine for another. All that is sensible is to look for the constantly more nearly complete use of the technical resources by means of a constantly more profound understanding of them, and aiming at the acquisition of the consequent new instrumental aptitudes. Until this is developed, the marvelous orchestra of the movies will continue to be played poorly, just as when a great concert piano is played by a baby's stiff fingers.

6. *The Radio*

~~~~~~

THE radio is an instrument of musical reproduction, but not in the same sense as the others already mentioned. The phonograph, the photography of sound, and the roll instruments reproduce a piece of music often in a given place, while the radio reproduces a sound instantly, transmitting it to all parts of the earth.

The general set-up for broadcasting is fundamentally the same as that for making records and for the photography of sound. The only difference is that the current coming from the microphone, instead of activating some recording apparatus, is transformed into Hertzian electric waves which travel through space at fabulous speeds. On being captured, these waves produce equivalent variations in an electric current, which vibrates the loudspeaker.

It is clear that all that has been said about wired transmission and its great musical possibilities also applies to the radio just as it does to the photography of sound, disc recording, and all the media which, in order to take in, modulate, and reprod::ce sound, use microphones, amplifiers, and loudspeakers. Disregarding certain technical imperfections which the radio still has, and which I shall not go into here, I want to speak of various effects the broadcasting of music has had on the social and cultural order.

One of the most important results of musical broadcasting is, as is well known, the gigantic increase in the size of the audience of a performance. If the music public will not increase in numbers as the reach of a single performance thus increases, the number of performances will consequently be considerably reduced, as will the number of performers needed to play them. This reduction is caused not only by the radio, but also by the other reproducing instruments already treated. The proportion in which the necessity for original performances decreases in relation to the efficiency and development of reproductions cannot easily be fixed. This is a very complex phenomenon which, to be thoroughly studied, requires a special attention I shall not give it here. For the moment, all that interests us is the widely recognized fact that the development of all the necessary means of reproduction has enormously limited the number of orchestras and musicians in theaters, movie-houses, concert-halls, and other public places.

What is important to note is that this diminution in orchestras has produced a violent lack of balance.

It has caused a serious labor problem. Professional musicians who earn their livelihood by playing find themselves summarily dismissed. A single orchestra, playing in Hollywood for films, does the work of hundreds of orchestras formerly in movie-theaters in thousands of small cities.

The first idea that occurred to the musicians' unions was that they should oppose the development of electric apparatus, obtaining from governments regulations prohibiting its use, and thus re-establish in their posts the musicians and orchestras who had been dismissed. This attitude of the "machine-destroyers" is illogical and unscientific. It is impossible to oppose the development of human thought. Nothing authorizes a sensible rebellion against the machine.

This problem has not come up only in the field of music. It is the same as that of all artisans and workers in relation to mechanization. Machines make the work of man, of one man let us say, more effective. For this reason, when one man is sufficient the rest become unnecessary, and must be dismissed. Machines are not the enemies of man. The tragedy of millions of jobless workers was not caused by machines, but by the few individuals who own them and use them for their own exclusive profit.

In Mexico, I had occasion to deal with this problem with the Union of Musicians, who saw their situation collapsing. It was impossible, in those years of lively excitement, to convince them that their problem could not be attacked by obtaining protective legislation or by attempting to delay the development of the reproducing apparatus. I tried to convince my co-workers that all we could sensibly consider was the following: All the reproductive musical apparatus augment the value of a single direct performance. That is, a reproducer makes unnecessary all the other direct performances which it replaces. It is logical to conclude that, if a single performance will have this great value, with detrimental results to the others, a process of selection must naturally occur. The orchestra which survives will absorb the best instrumentalists available. The process of selection will continually become more acute. Young students will gain entry into professional circles—constantly more limited—by excelling the quality of those already inside, who, in turn, will be able to prevent the new recruits from entering only by not allowing their own quality to be excelled.

Nobody can successfully oppose such a phenomenon of selection. There will remain only the problem of the unemployed, a great social problem which better political and economic organizations than ours must some day solve satisfactorily for all workers. Until a general readjustment of work is achieved, we shall have to suffer the consequences of a transition, and fight for a regime equitable in its division of work. Certainly the principle of the division of labor will not become active arbitrarily. It will conform, in the future, to the vocational inclinations of the individual, as a function of the social need for balanced production and consumption. There is no reason to fear the development of the machine. In such a regime of divided labor, all men will be occupied, and machines will no longer be at the command of a few individuals, being in the service of all.

The radio has weeded out the field of musical labor. The most able musicians have remained, the least able have had to be eliminated. By precipitating this labor problem, by causing such a selective process, by transmitting the music of a given performance to all parts of the world simultaneously, the radio becomes an undreamed-of means for distributing the art of music among the people of the world.

Music is a satisfaction related to an expressive, nervous—aesthetic, if you will—need as important and undeniable as the necessity for shelter which has brought with it its corresponding satisfaction, clothing and the house. Music should circulate, be distributed as water, for example, today comes to everyone. It should, like urbanization and hygiene in the hands of an ideal state, flow easily to the diverse components of society. At present, it is distributed as a part of general education—primary, secondary, or superior—which is a duty of the state, and in the form of concerts and other public musical spectacles.

Going as far back into history as possible, we see that music has always occupied a prominent place among human manifestations. Associated with war, poetry, dancing, the theater, magic rites and religious cults, or as a language of sentiments and emotions, it has appeared among all peoples at all times in human history as an irreplaceable practice. In each epoch it has been practiced in a different way. It has been produced and circulated in diverse ways, depending on the general characteristics of society.

The Concert

In the past century, aside from church music, street music, and so-called salon music, our flourishing European cities developed the public concert as a general form of musical distribution. The concert brought together varied publics, and put the music of cultivated artists within the reach of many social groups to whom it had long been denied. European courts of the eighteenth century stimulated the production of new types of music, which for many years were the exclusive privilege of Maecenases and patrons. By facilitating the gathering of varied audiences, the concert made possible a concentration of music of very diverse origins: chamber and symphonic music, patronized by the courts and their Maecenases; religious music—now taken out of the churches; and the music of aristocratic salons. Very soon the concert developed a new sort of music, one in accord with its own characteristics, a kind of pyrotechnic music related to the large apparatus of exhibitionism which the concert itself is. Beyond question, an unequivocal typical case of this class of "concert music" is the larger part of Franz Liszt's production. Finally, the concert drew into itself the popular music of street and field, in the form of more or less appropriate concert arrangements.

Judged as a whole, the concert is a typically "liberal" institution, which consequently was given extraordinary vitality when liberal thought produced the great development of the bourgeoisie. To complete the picture of the typically bourgeois characteristics of the concert, only the financial side is missing: (1) an admission charge, varying with the accommodations in the hall, and grouping the audience into their classes, and (2) a financial return to the artist and impresario, converting the artistic product into a material of commerce. At the beginning of this century, the concert achieved a flowering which it seemed impossible to interrupt. But new and unlooked-for developments intervened.

The mechanical means of musical reproduction we

have been studying have brought with them a radical change in the manner, form, and extension of the distribution of music. The radio takes music out of the concert hall and puts it into the air, in all the space surrounding our planet, in such a way that anyone with a relatively simple apparatus can hear it.

The concert has been seriously affected, and even shows symptoms of obvious decadence. But this is no sign that it must or should disappear, killed by the new means of musical reproduction. I think, rather, that of the concert there will persist the part which is characteristic, and which has not as yet been replaced by other means. The concert will undoubtedly have to undergo a transformation, the details of which it is impossible to predict.

Radio and the Concert

Those of us who have gone frequently to bullfights know that the great attraction of the *fiesta* does not lie solely in the bulls being good and the *toreros* performing good *faenas*. It lies also in the individual feeling of each spectator as part of an enthusiastic group eager for emotion. The nervous system of the individual functions differently when he is alone and when he is part of a large mass of individuals. His whole general attitude, receptive capacity, and sensibility are different. Boxing also proves this. It is not the same to hear a prizefight reported by radio as it is to be part of the deliriously enthusiastic multitude ardently following the course of a sensational fight.

The concert has a social value (social in the good sense of the word) which the radio does not have. Furthermore, the two institutions are opposite in that the concert tends to bring people together, the radio to isolate them from each other. Large human concourses at concerts, performances, and artistic festivals have a psychological interest and value which nothing seems to diminish. Furthermore, the artist and the public establish a current of sympathy beneficial to both. We see this not only in our bourgeois spectacles, but also in the case of some popular artists at fairs who, in their monologues, mimicry, and music, fascinate the multitudes to a point beyond mere diversion.

This has stimulated the exhibitionism and stultification of many virtuosi who forget their legitimate function as interpreters in attempting to impress their listeners at any cost. It goes without saying that the plague of this type of virtuoso should be destroyed. But, not to expand on this point, it is well to make clear that the radio has made more obvious than ever the capacity of an artist to establish in the concert-hall a current of true and proper understanding with the public. By radio we can hear good music well played. In the concert-hall, this is not enough. The listener wants to have a sensation of communication corresponding to man's natural social tendencies. One of the undeniable effects of the radio is to promote the process of selection, by means of which the "cold" interpreters are disappearing and the inspired ones obtaining constantly greater validity. This explains the constantly more open rebuffs which the public has been giving the German *Kappelmeisters*.

It has often been said that the greatest merit of a performer is that he does not interpret the music, but merely reveals the composer's intentions. This claim can never be made on a firm basis, as was said in an earlier chapter. For me, the great merit of an interpretive performer is precisely in that he does interpret the music, but interprets it well, using his personal capacity to re-create during the performance the music which lies inert on the paper, as well as using his own power of convincing the public.

The contact between the artist and the public, so necessary to the perfect consummation of the musical process, produced simply and spontaneously in good concerts, cannot be produced directly with the material means of the radio. There is, however, an indirect contact which by itself seems to be attempting easier channels and more efficient resources. The so-called "reports"—by telephone, telegraph, and mail —are an expression of the natural need for this contact between the performer and the public. On the other hand, the development a radio artist gains through his correct feeling of the listeners has undoubtedly reached a considerable height.

Facing a microphone, it is possible to feel the presence of the listeners with great intensity. This feeling has undoubtedly had an effect on the performer even though he has an always unknown and invisible audience. Until now, a view of the public, and its presence in the same place, have been the conditions and considerations most favorable to making an artist feel his contact with the public. This does not mean, however, that there cannot exist other conditions equally good, or perhaps even better, in the case of the radio. It is impossible to predict anything. Unquestionably, the mere knowledge that there is a numerous audience scattered over a large part of the earth, for which the broadcast will be useful and satisfying, gives the radio artist highly stimulating encouragement and satisfaction.

Radio as a Means of Distribution

There has never been a better instrument than the radio for bringing to all men the benefits of scientific and artistic culture. What is needed to spread them effectively is the most complete and profitable use of the radio. Up to the present, broadcasting has been done by two agents, the state and business. In countries like Mexico, in which commercial broadcasting exists, the radio has been exploited by private enterprises for commercial purposes. In some European countries, the radio is a state monopoly, managed like any other public service—and for preponderantly educational purposes. In both cases, the radio has proved an excellent instrument for propagating art and ideas of every kind. What the broadcasting organizations still have not done is to develop the methods of work, the artistic and literary creations native to the new physical means, and related to a purpose definitely educational in the fullest sense of the word.

At the present time, the radio is invading the fields of the daily press, the book, the theater, the school, the concert-hall, the religious and political platform —not with its own methods, but simply transplanting the ancient ones. I think that the radio, in order completely to achieve its high cultural ends, must be complemented in some form guaranteeing not only a good broadcast but a fruitful reception on the part of the public. I often think that at present the radio is frequently, at best, a voice speaking well, but not understood, or imperfectly understood, or heard inopportunely.

One proof that the radio has not developed its own methods is found in its musical practices. What has been sought is not how to make the best music for the radio, but the best means of making the radio transmit music which already exists. The great creative genius of the engineers who have developed the radio has not yet been equaled by the artists, educators, or administrators.

The Radio and Musical Creation

If engineers constantly seek the perfection of instrumental means, the musicians ought to seek the constant development of related new expressions. But this cannot be a labor independently done by artists for pure idealism. It must be done in relation to the great broadcasting organizations, which have left lamentable gaps in this department. Strong and powerful as social institutions, and backed by tremendous economic force, they have not kept in mind that the stimulation and sustenance of artistic creation are to their own interest. It is time to drop the idea that to sustain composers is to give charity or merely perform a grand gesture. The Maecenases did not— and do not—perform acts of generosity. They perform deficiently a social function imposed on them as an obligation by their own economic status. The administrators of radio, in their own interest, ought to support composers, just as they sustain research engineers to produce the scientific advance. Sooner or later this must be understood not only by radio executives and impresarios, but by the composers themselves, who will consequently change their attitude and live in a worthier and more secure position.

For research in, and establishment of, the practices related to the pick-up and mixing—to cite two specific cases—the constant collaboration of musicians is as essential as that of engineers. At present, during the best broadcasts of the finest orchestras of the United States, the expert in charge of the mixing panel does as much or more for the sound-balance of the music broadcast as does the director himself.

We are used to thinking that the places in which composers start and are educated are conservatories and music-schools. Speaking in general terms, the conservatory has been good for developing performing musicians, but has not been exactly the place in which the great composers, the masters of music, have been formed. They have never, in reality, needed a school properly speaking, with its conventional organization, plan of studies divided into years or grades at the close of which there are examinations, etc., etc. The great masters of music have developed their natural faculties in the practice of music itself. Händel was not only a composer writing his works down on paper; he lived the life of the theater. He himself was an impresario. He wrote his operas for immediate performance. He lived in the orchestra, in the theater, in the whole organization of the musical life of his time. Bach was a religious composer because he lived in the Church, from the Church, and for the Church. He wrote chorales, oratorios, motets, masses, and cantatas—which were needed for the Church's services. He wrote for the organ because it was the Church instrument and because it was the instrument at hand, the one he had to play. When he was in Cöthen, he had a different function, with other instruments at hand. Then his music was for instruments (*Brandenburg Concerti*) and for use in teaching, as he himself was a professor of clavichord (whence the origin of *The Well-Tempered Clavichord*). Nor need it be said that the composers of the Roman Catholic Church were always formed in the atmosphere and constant practice of religious music.

The conservatories and schools of music, even though they may give their students of composition a theoretical instruction (necessarily static) of more or less breadth, do not provide the composer with the real stage for his work. They do not provide practical resources for his work, for the simple reason that their function is not to practice music, but to teach the theoretical part of it. It is in this sense that the schools for composers foment the sterile ivory-tower attitude which creates musicians on a theoretical level. History shows that all the great masters of music constantly perfected their art through practice, that they always wrote for public performance, that their music—however revolutionary it was considered in its day—responded to a demand and had commercial value to publishers and managers.

The esteem in which great artists are held grows constantly after their deaths, but we do not know of a single Bach unknown in his lifetime, but discovered and glorified after his death. Great composers never learned their art in an ivory tower, but in its constant practice. At the present time the conservatories and schools of music cannot provide the proper surroundings for the development of the great composers of today. On the other hand, the policy of the great radio organizations consists of providing only the means of musical performance. This will one day inevitably lead to a shortage of adequate repertoire which will be a serious problem.

The radio, as the social institution of our day controlling the whole musical movement, should see that one of the important departments of its organization ought to include the means needed for the production of new musical creations. The whole structure of musical activity will undergo a gigantic transformation because of the radio. We must reach a point from which we can get the whole perspective. This is exactly what interests me more and more in an attempt at a general interpretation of the effects which the great achievements of electromechanics will have on the music of the present.

7. *Electric Apparatus of Sound Production*

IN the preceding chapters, we have spoken of the various mechanisms which make musical reproduction possible. The roll is a mechanical means of operating a musical instrument (piano, organ, violin, etc.) with the greatest precision, and identically as often as desired. The phonograph and sound photography store up with increasing perfection a given performance by voices or musical instruments. The radio reproduces a performance, making it available in all parts of the world at once. Finally, we shall now look at the case of the instruments on which the production of sound itself is obtained by electric means.

Up to now, the sound-agents have been (a) strings (families of violins and lutes), (b) columns of air (families of woodwinds and brasses), and (c) plates and membranes (so-called percussion instruments). The procedures for obtaining vibrations from them have been, in general terms, (a) rubbing (violins), (b) blowing (wind instruments), (c) striking (piano

138

and other percussion instruments), and (d) plucking (harps and lutes).

The group of instruments in the modern symphony orchestra is substantially the same as that which, thousands of years ago, formed the Egyptian, Assyrian, and Chinese orchestras. Going as far back in history as possible, we find peoples living five thousand years B.C. using the same sound-agents we use today, and vibrating them by the same means. With the exception of bowed strings (violins), about whose history there is still much controversy, instruments have the same general form and constituent parts they had then. The *nabla,* an Egyptian lute, contained a sounding box, neck, frets, pegs, bridge, and strings. The harps also contained all the essential elements. The wind instruments were (a) *a bec* (family of flutes), (b) with round mouthpieces (family of trumpets), and (c) of double and single reed (family of oboes and clarinets, respectively). The percussion instruments were simply the same: tympani, cymbals, castanets, crotals, tambourines, etc.

This means, in a few words, that musical instruments have not changed substantially in seven thousand years. In the course of this long period of time there has been great improvement in the construction and playing of the instruments, so that we now have far better control of them than was possible in remote antiquity. But during seventy centuries there did not appear a single musical instrument containing a new sound-agent, or showing a new procedure of vibrating its agent. We received our present sound-material complete from pre-history. Electric instruments of sound production offer the first case in history of a new musical instrument. They contain (a) a new sound-agent, (b) a new manner of vibrating that agent, and (c) a new means of controlling that vibration—in frequency (pitch), amplitude (intensity), and form (timbre).

Since we learned our elementary physics we have known that musical sound is a vibration produced by a sound-agent and transmitted to our ears by the air. The varying frequency of the vibrations produces different heights of sound (*pitch*); the differing amplitude of the vibrations produces greater or less *intensity*; the larger or smaller quantity of harmonics which appear, as well as their varying relative intensity, produce variety in the *timbre*.

The sound-agent in the electric apparatus of sound production is an alternating electric current. This current always has a given frequency which is converted into acoustic energy when connected to the loudspeaker. This, in turn, produces a sound of frequency equal to that of the current. It is clear, then, that in this case the sound-agent and the manner of vibrating it are practically the same thing: the electric current is in itself a vibration which becomes acoustic vibration in the loudspeaker. This is why the means of controlling the vibration is perfect. Through the usual systems of electrodynamics it is possible to produce alternating currents of a desired frequency. The way, then, of obtaining a sound of a determined pitch— for example the *la* of four hundred forty vibrations per second—is to produce an alternating current of equal frequency. Greater frequencies correspond to higher sounds, lesser frequencies to lower sounds. Through this procedure tuning ceases to be a problem. All desired sounds can be obtained with complete exactness. It will not be a problem to produce sounds in quarter- or sixth-tones, as two sounds can be produced of, say, as little difference as four hundred forty and four hundred forty-one vibrations per second respectively.

The intensity of sound can be obtained with no limitation other than that imposed by our hearing organs. By the same amplifying systems already mentioned in previous chapters, the fullness of the alternating current can be graduated at will. The continuous duration of the sound can be infinite—there are no lungs to tire or bows to snap.

Finally, these electric apparatus have solved the problem of controlling timbre in a perfect and admirable manner. A vibration is an isochronic movement, like that of a pendulum, which is graphically represented by a sinusoidal wave such as appears on

Drawing 8. This is what is called a simple vibration. But the vibrations of a sounding-body are never simple, but are composites of various vibrations. The so-called musical sound is a composite of many concomitant vibrations, also called harmonics, as expressed in the following musical notation:

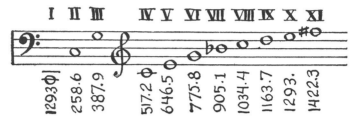

For a clearer understanding of this phenomenon, I want to indicate in Drawing 8 the simple vibrations of the 1st, 2nd, 3rd, and 4th harmonics by the sinusoids A, B, C, and D. The curve indicated in E is the result of the four previous sinusoids, and represents graphically the form of the vibration which produces the musical sound composed of the four harmonics cited. The intensity of each one of the harmonics which form this group is different. The first—called the fundamental harmonic—is always heard with greater intensity than any other. The others have varying intensities. The so-called timbre of sound depends on the greater or less number of harmonics produced, and their relative intensities. On the oboe, for example, the high harmonics are very intense,

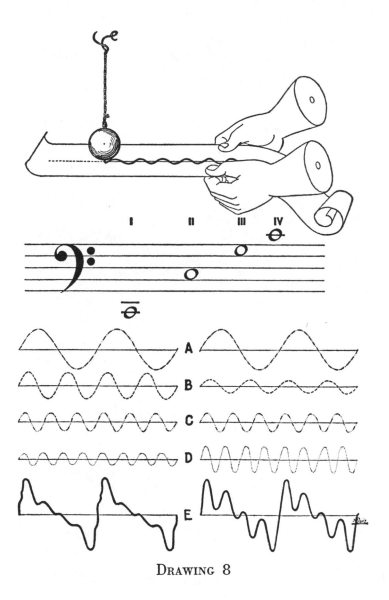

DRAWING 8

while on the horn the greater richness is in the low harmonics.

The effect of the difference in relative intensity of the harmonics can also be appreciated graphically in Drawing 8. Two columns of sinusoids appear, A, B, C, and D. In the left-hand column, the intensity (amplitude of vibration) of the 2nd harmonic is greater than that of the 4th. In the right-hand column, the intensity of the 4th harmonic is greater than that of the 2nd, the 1st and 3rd being equal. The difference produced by this diverse degree of intensity of the harmonics indicated can be seen graphically in the resulting E.

Electricity, by simple means, can fix the height and intensity of electric sound with exact precision. It can, furthermore, mix all the vibrations of distinct frequency (height) and amplitude (intensity) desired. It is consequently possible to fix the timbre of sound with complete precision. Timbre ceases to be a fixed and particular value of each instrument, and becomes a quality of sound which musical creation should fix, as it fixes rhythm, intensity and duration of sounds. By being able so perfectly to dominate the primary qualities of sound—*pitch, intensity, duration,* and *timbre*—we obtain the augmentation of other secondary resources or qualities, not of sound, but of music. That is to say, of scales, harmony, sound-balance, harmonic coloring, etc.

Scales

The successions of sounds used in music have not been established by chance. Man, in the first place, has in his throat an organ of limited resources, varying in the male from 80 to 6,300 vibrations a second, and in the female from 190 to 9,200. Primitive man intuitively found those sounds which went best with others. He admitted that the sound which goes best with another is its double, or octave; then its fifth, fourth, etc. In this way man established a fixed series of sounds formed by those which he found to have the greatest natural relationship. This is what we call a scale. The oldest scales of which we have knowledge are built on the consonances commonly called natural (octave and fifth) which also serve as the basis of the diatonic scale, fundamental in our present occidental system of music. The Greeks were the first to express the relations of sounds with numbers. They found that a given string, when divided in half, produced exactly the higher octave, and therefore they expressed this relation by 1:2; the fifth by 2:3; the fourth by 3:4, etc. This act made clear and scientifically explained what had been found by all previous peoples.

This teaches us that the scales have a physical foundation perfectly concordant with human nature, and that consequently nobody can fix fundamental scales arbitrarily. We nevertheless find in the course of history a movement toward scales containing new intervals. The Renaissance consolidated so-called chromaticism. It is worth noting that this was not produced with the desire of seeking new intervals and more divisions in the octave. Chromaticism was in reality a conquence of the various systems of transposition which aimed at nothing more than repeating one diatonic scale, but beginning it on a different note.

The chromatic scale is not in itself a melodic scale, but a means of making possible a sequence of diatonic scales beginning on various tonics. Nevertheless its existence in itself has caused the discovery of its proper melodic feeling and the founding of its relative twelve-tone harmony. This latter we could properly call chromaticism (as opposed to diatonicism), that is to say, that which considers the twelve-tone scale and all the accords possible to produce with it in its own expressive sense, and which has no relation to the diatonic scale and its accords.

The Hindu scale of twenty-two sounds in the double is another case of the tendency toward small intervals. It is well to keep in mind that the Hindu scale, despite making this division into small intervals, has as its fundamental basis the scale formed of the notes *sa ri ga ma pa da ni,* which is unmistakably diatonic.

Observation of the widely varying oriental systems

of scales allows us to draw the conclusion that all existing scales are fundamentally diatonic, of the seven sounds originating in the series of six fifths:

This scale always was preceded by the pentatonic scale of six semitones (pentatonic diatonic) originating in the series of four fifths:

But in many cases the incidental presence of "chromatic" intervals came to alter almost completely the diatonic feeling. Examples are—to cite only the most important—the system of Greek *genera*, that of the Hindu *srutis* already cited, and the very rich variety of Arab scales. So it is that, even if the scales of all peoples have a diatonic core, we can notice a constant movement toward intervals smaller than the whole tone.

In this connection, we should also refer to the attemps to divide the double into intervals smaller than the semitone which, from time to time since the seventeenth century, some musicians and musical theorists have made. These have had the purpose of achieving greater melodic richness and of solving the problem of establishing more adequate "temperaments" than that of twelve sounds now in use. The search for scales with constantly smaller intervals will continue, but does not necessarily mean the discarding of the fundamental intervals of the octave, fifth, fourth, etc. The notion of consonance will thus continue to evolve.

The concept of consonance and dissonance has evolved in the same feeling as affects the intervals in the series of harmonics. It happens that, as the sounds in the series get farther from the fundamental, they have a more remote relationship among themselves. The relationship in first degree is the octave, in second degree the fifth, then the fourth, major third, minor third, major second, minor second, etc., as can be seen in the scale itself:

The degrees of consonance of two distinct notes, in the order in which the intervals appear in the natural series of harmonics (without counting inversions), are the following:

1st degree of consonance: perfect fifth (from 2nd
to 3rd)

2nd degree of consonance: major third (from 4th
to 5th)

3rd degree of consonance: minor third (from 5th
to 6th)

4th degree of consonance: major second (from 7th
to 8th)

5th degree of consonance: minor second (from
11th to 12th)

etc., etc., or perfect fifth, major third, minor third,
major second, minor second, etc., etc.

The Greeks liked the fifth and fourth, and did not
allow the dissonance of a third, which was accepted
during the Middle Ages with the *faux-bourdon*. It was
not until the seventeenth and eighteenth centuries that
the major second and its inversion, the minor seventh,
were admitted. The minor second and its inversion,
the major seventh, were not taken in until the
twentieth century. The historic progress of the concept
of consonance, then, is identical with the successive
order of consonances in the scale of natural harmonics:

perfect fifth . . . . Greece (polyphony)
major and minor thirds. . . Middle   Ages   (*faux-
                             bourdon,* twelfth and
                             thirteenth centuries)

major second . . . . seventeenth and eighteenth centuries
minor second . . . . twentieth century
etc., etc.

Nobody can say with justice that consonance is an absolute value. It is simply a truth relative to each epoch. The foregoing authorizes us to confirm the idea that in the future it will continue evolving toward smaller intervals, since the creative impulse of the individual can never be stopped. This evolution can take place only through the establishment of new temperaments, that is to say, new scales of fixed sounds providing not only intervals smaller than the smallest now in use, but also permitting progress in the conquest of pure intervals, so-called physical intervals such as appear in the natural phenomenon of the series of harmonics.

To clarify this concept a little, it will be good to have an idea, however general, of what a tempered scale is. The temperament of twelve sounds now in use is made to serve the interests of the diatonic scale of seven tones. Its object is to form a fixed series or scale in which the principal intervals obtain with the slightest possible deformation. For example, a series of twelve fifths provides a sound differing by a Pythagorean comma from that provided in a series of seven octaves:

In order to make a system of fixed sounds providing the pure intervals of the perfect fifth and octave, we should have to include a fabulous number of sounds differing only in the slightest degree from each other. Notice further that so tremendous a complication would have as its only object that of preserving the purity of the octaves and fifths, which are, moreover, the most elemental consonances (harmonics 2 and 3). Such a temperament is a practical impossibility.

For this reason there was conceived the division of the differences of the sounds which resulted from series of octaves and fifths and the establishment of a single sound which would serve as the result of octaves and fifths. If we were to try to achieve purity in the intervals proceeding from the 5th, 7th, 9th, 11th, 13th, etc., harmonics, the complications would become fantastic. Nevertheless, the tendency is unquestionably in that direction. There can be no doubt that the widely varied melodic shiftings and the so-called exotic harmonies of the Arabs, the Hindus, and many American indigenes are a manifestation of their intuitive search for the musical expression of the intervals corresponding to the high harmonics of the scale of concomitant sounds.

But in order to arrive at new, richer, and more perfect temperaments, practical mechanical means are required. It is not possible to obtain them with our pianos, violins, and saxophones. It is necessary to have instruments which can be tuned with all precision in the new scales, and which can be played easily. The electric instruments of sound production offer the satisfactory solution to this problem, for— as was explained above—they have the capacity to fix and maintain the height of the sound with all precision. As will be seen later, the establishment of new scales brings with it as a consequence an extraordinary augmentation of the harmonic resources of musical art.

Melody and Harmony

Each particular case of a scale (successive or melodic series of sounds) brings with it a particular case of harmony (simultaneous series of sounds). I think that the melodic complexion of music provides its own proper relative harmonic complexion. In the same way that successive series of visual images

persist on our retina, so also series of successive
sounds persist in our auditory organs, forming accords. If we hear a scale played on a piano: *do, re,
mi,* etc., we cannot say that when the *re* is vibrating
we have lost the auditory notion of the *do,* and so on.
On the other hand, even if the instrument has cut off
the vibration of the first sound before producing the
second, the vibration of the first stays in the air for
many instants.

In view of this undeniable fact, the affirmation
that in antiquity primitive peoples did not know of
harmony has always seemed to me naïve. Imagine a
melody played on a lyre or harp, and remember its
resonance. Thus also the very ancient pentaphonic
chimes of the Chinese!

Every harmonic system, formulated or not, comes
out of the intervals melodically produced in the scale.
Thus, in historic order, the scales provide their own
harmony based exclusively on the intervals they
contain:

PENTAPHONIC SCALE

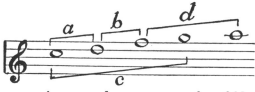

a. major second   c. perfect fifth
b. minor third   d. major third
          plus their inversions.

EXAPHONIC SCALE BY TONES

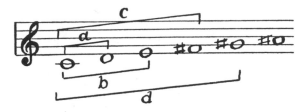

a. major second
b. major third
c. augmented fourth
d. augmented fifth   plus their inversions and enharmonics.

THE MAJOR DIATONIC SCALE

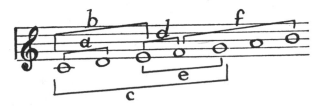

a. major second
b. major third
c. perfect fifth
d. minor second
e. minor third
f. augmented fourth   plus their inversions.

THE TEMPERED SCALE OF TWELVE TONES

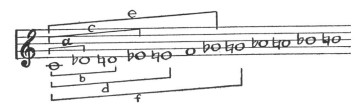

a. minor second
b. major second
c. minor third
d. major third
e. diminished fifth
f. perfect fifth plus their inversions and enharmonics.

This observation is borne out by abundant examples taken from the music of the Mexican and Peruvian Indians in the case of the pentaphonic scales, and that of contemporary Central European composers in the case of music on the twelve tones. Also, from historic observation it is possible not only to make the positive affirmation that the melodic intervals of the scales are the basis of the harmonic intervals, but also its opposite: no harmonic intervals exist which are not also contained melodically in the scale.

Within the diatonic harmony there is produced a well-known phenomenon, by which there are recognized in each step of the scale what are called tonal functions. They consist, fundamentally, in the sensation of repose felt in the initial note of the tonic scale, and in the movement prevailing in the fifth or dominant note. The other notes of the scale are subsidiary to the dominant's tendency of movement. When a tonality is established, successions of sounds are produced which are called for by the force of these tendencies. These successions form what is called a cadence. Concretely, we could say: Cadence is a succession of sounds established by the strength of the tonal functions of the steps of the diatonic scale. For example:

It might be thought at first sight that this phenomenon of cadence, so important in diatonic music, is par excellence harmonic and has nothing to do with the melodic constitution of the system of sounds. But a profound observation of the phenomenon will show with clarity that the so-called tonal function is not an harmonic phenomenon, but melodic par excellence: the attraction is from note to note, by melodic intervals, as can be proved in the series mentioned:

minor second; major second; minor third; major third; perfect fifth.

The effect of the accord on each one of these steps is only to reinforce it, just as the harmonics reinforce their fundamental in the natural phenomenon of the vibration of sounding bodies. Look at the following successions in cadence, one to the dominant, the other to the tonic:

This is not the place to enter into greater details in regard to this matter. I have wanted only to give a general idea of the melodic foundation of tonal functions, in order to prove once more that an harmonic system depends on its related system of melody or scale. When the necessary development of instruments is achieved, melodic systems will evolve toward smaller intervals, fixing themselves in new and richer temperaments. Harmony will then continue ascending toward the peaks of the scale of natural harmonics.

Sound Balance

The modern symphony orchestra is the most nearly universal and varied that can be imagined. The instruments of all epochs and regions have not been united in this ensemble for eclectic reasons, but because of the natural march of historic events, and as a result of the influences of civilizations on each other. It is easy to observe evidence of the contrasts in a symphony orchestra at first sight. But to give a general idea of the different possibilities of the instruments in the orchestra as regards sound-volume, it will be enough to remember some general principles at the basis of classic orchestration:

I. Each instrument has three clearly distinct registers: (a) the deep register (dark), (b) the middle register, and (c) the high register (brilliant). The difficulty, in general, is to play *forte* in the deep register, and to play *piano* in the high.

II. The sound-capacity of an instrument is evaluated in relation to the strength of the same instruments playing at the same time, *e.g.*, one trumpet = two horns = four clarinets. This principle is valid only when all the instruments play in the same register.

I have mentioned these two cases because it is impossible to enter into detailed consideration of the art of compensating sounds, and merely to give some idea of the fact that, in the symphony orchestra, the sound-planes are fixed by the established limitations of each particular instrument. The conditions of the sound-material of the modern symphony orchestra, with volume-capacities so different in each family, each instrument, each register of each instrument, have caused the genius of the artists to reach constantly higher planes in order to conquer such violent contrasts, and to take advantage of such dissimilar resources. Certainly the fascinating beauty of our orchestra comes, in great part, from its heterogeneous and contrasted nature.

Nevertheless, the genius of men will be able to do more when the disparity of available resources is not imposed, when they themselves can obtain both violent contrasts and gradual changes. An orchestra of electric instruments can obtain—in all the timbres, all the registers and durations—the degree of volume desired, and with no limitation whatsoever. Using the material means to obtain gradual change in sonority does not exclude the possibility of using all the contrasts conceived by the imagination. With such new resources, the sound-planes in a musical work will reach a relative proportion now inconceivable.

The Harmony of Timbres

The similar disparity patent in the timbre of the various instruments in the symphony orchestra has also preoccupied many musicians and famous writers. They have dealt with the fact that there is a large gap between the timbre of string instruments and wind in-

struments, and in the latter group between woodwinds
and brasses. European instrument-makers of the past
century tried to fill in these gaps, and for a long time
it was hoped that the saxophones would be the needed
bridge between the woodwinds and the brasses. Also,
certain established formulae of instrumental combina-
tions were spoken of, with which there were attempted
those amalgams and composite timbres which might
link the sharpest contrasts. As a matter of fact, however, the situation did not change.

The harmony which sounds should have among
themselves with respect to timbre is a musical quality
as important as that we usually refer to as harmony
—which refers to the relations of sounds of different
pitches. The advances to be made by means of scientific and artistic speculations with relation to the harmony of timbre are incalculable. The importance of
this point would award it not a separate chapter, but
an entire book.

Let us remember that timbre is a quality of sounds
in their "harmonic" relations properly speaking. We
said that timbre is determined by the quantity of
harmonics which appear together with the fundamental, as well as by the special intensity with which
each of them is present. It has also been said that, as
a consequence, the possibility of precisely controlling
the various degrees of volume and pitch, as well as
of mixing various sounds to form a single one, gives

us the power to produce an infinite number of musical timbres. With this achievement, music has seen its media enriched as never before. The control of the timbre of sound is equal to nothing less than having invented an infinite number of new musical instruments.

The Present Status of the Electric Apparatus of Sound Production

In the preceding paragraphs, I have wanted to refer to the fact that the art of music is widened by the mere possibility of easily and exactly determining the height, intensity, and timbre of sound, and have not especially considered the means by which this is to be done. It should be clearly understood that the advantages for music in being able to use all the possible tempered scales, the complete gradation of musical timbres, the complete palette of sound-intensities, etc., do not come specifically from electricity, but from the fact that electric media make it possible to dominate and control sound-vibrations.

Let us take a look at the present state of the electric apparatus of sound production, and acquaint ourselves with their degree of practicability as instruments destined to actual use in musical art. It is one thing that an apparatus exists capable of producing sounds with all possible physical conditions, and another to invent an instrument taking advantage of these same physical conquests, making actual musical performances possible.

About a dozen distinguished investigators have worked on the starting and advance of these apparatus. The apparatus of Theremin and the Hammond organ are already well known. It is impossible at this moment to give any opinion as to what would be the best manner of giving musical performances, properly speaking, on electric instruments. This problem can be solved only by long experimentation. We can say, however, that the simplicity of electric operation will permit the invention of new forms of keyboards. The form and placing of the keyboards now in use are in fundamental relation to the anatomic configuration of the hand. In the case of the piano, which is the most important keyboard instrument, the complexity of the system of hammers has prevented new dispositions of the keyboard, which might otherwise exist.

It is unquestionable that the means practiced by Theremin do not throw any new light on the problem. His so-called "space control" instrument has no practical advantages. It has various major inconveniences. One is the difficulty of fixing the pitch, which imposes a limitation of always using slow melodic successions. Another is the inevitable *portamento* between a sound and the one following it, however much the first can be more or less violently deadened. A third is that the "attack" always is imperfect and awkward. We must think of the great richness, variety and elasticity of the attack on many traditional instruments in order to see clearly the great difficulty of this problem of the performance of electric instruments—the enormous richness of the *coups d'archet,* of so-called "touches" on the piano, the widely varied attacks on the instruments with mouthpieces—in which the *embouchure* and the inflections of the breath produce an infinite variety.

To me, this seems at present one of the most difficult points to solve: to find a medium adequate to human anatomy, and taking advantage of the infinite facility of the electric production of sound. This refers to new instruments of direct performance. But there is also the possibility of working out new instruments operated mechanically by means of systems similar to those followed with automatic pianos and organs. The perspectives seem good in this direction. Furthermore, in this way man's anatomic limitations will cease to be also a limitation for music.

The solution of the problems related to musical practice with the new electric instruments has been considerably delayed because their inventors have not been aiming—as the first purpose of their labors and investigations—to promote the advance of the art of music. Even if they had, however, the inventors themselves do not understand musical problems and necessities. This shows the necessity for the inventors to interest themselves in the practical use of their inventions, or to associate themselves with musicians in pursuing their investigations.

I have had proof of this observation in the case of Theremin's instruments, which are clearly intended to imitate the traditional instruments. Furthermore, the sentimental melodies of the conventional repertoire are used to try them. I also remember having heard it said that one of the great advantages of these instruments is that everyone who wishes to can play them even though they do not know music! It is a great mistake to wish the new electric instruments to equal the traditional ones, since the latter already exist and are at hand.

Furthermore, it is naïve to wish to practice today's music on the new instruments. There is no object in playing on them music born on a violoncello, and which, consequently, no other instrument can play as well. There is no sense in making a new instrument for old music. The traditional music of today is perfectly fitted to its own instruments. The new instruments will produce an unforeseen music, as unlooked-for as the instruments themselves. Just as the physicists produced a new instrument, the musicians will produce a new music.

8. *Toward a New Music*

NOTHING is wholly new. Each thing, however new it appears, had many antecedents. It is often said that Bach was the father of music in the literal sense of the word. By this is meant that this great master gave life to something which did not exist. Many people believe this—some because of naïveté, others because of lack of information or attention. Bach would not have been Bach if Vivaldi, Buxtehude, and Luther had not lived before him. Luther, Buxtehude, and Vivaldi made the appearance of a Bach inevitable.

We nevertheless find in the constant evolution of music certain eras in which it has been possible to synthesize with great success conquests made in various subsidiary branches of the main trunk. Bach, for example, took advantage of the instrumental and theoretical advance reached in his own epoch with the clavichord, the pipe-organ, and temperament. In such epochs evolution has proceeded so rapidly as not to allow time to consider antecedents, and we therefore have an impression of spontaneously generated novelties. We should, then, keep this in mind when thinking of a new music, and not expect sudden revelations, disconnected from the past and from the general conditions of the present.

I speak of the possibility of a new music because there are at present in sight realizations both innumerable and varied, and because we have seen in the course of this book that new forms of art correspond to new physical means and new sociological circumstances. We are not, then, dealing with the art of a more or less distant future, but of the present in which we live. The artist should belong to his time, and has but one means of doing so: by steeping himself in history in order to extract from it the experience of past generations, and by knowing his own world with all its developments and resources, so that he may be able to interpret its own fundamental necessities.

After having glanced at the new instruments which today are within our reach, we might have some doubt of the possibility of an artist, in order to produce his new creations, dominating such complicated apparatus as the sound film, for example, in all its details. But let us note that the composer has always been capable of managing his mechanical instruments. If Chopin had not managed the piano as perfectly as he did, he would not have produced the marvelous

piano music we all know and admire. In the same
way, the composers who will make a true musical
drama of the cinema will be those who know how to
manage its various instrumentalities as perfectly as
Chopin dominated the piano.

In an earlier chapter we spoke of the way in which
an instrument develops a related instrumental aptitude in the individual. The exercise of the function
makes it become instinctive, and in this way it will
come about that the new instruments will be at our
command, as useful and natural as our voice and
hands. If we look at the problem implied for the composer in conceiving a complex filmed music drama,
we find that it is, in different manner and degree, the
same problem presented in the case of an opera or a
symphony: that of familiarizing himself with the instrumental means. In a classic symphony, each musical part is decided in relation to the instrumental
possibility. The part played by the violin fits that instrument, and is inappropriate for the tuba. This
propriety of music in relation to the instrument which
produces it is what a musician means when he talks
about a violinistic, unviolinistic, pianistic, or un-
pianistic passage.

A composer who knew only the mechanism of the
violin would be unable to write for orchestra or opera.
It may seem too difficult, this achieving of an understanding of very varied and complex mechanisms, but

intellect and practice make it possible. In the particular case of the cinema, the new "apprenticeship" will not begin while musicians continue making only adaptations. The musical adaptations for cinematographic films are not more or less satisfactory than any other adaptation. Every adaptation implies the use of a thing originally conceived for another purpose. The music of *Tristan* fits that opera better than any other.

The dreadful salads of sections of classic works, sentimental melodies, and popular songs which are generally confected to accompany films prove nothing but the inability of producers to conceive original cinematographic works with their own music. The same thing happened in the seventeenth and eighteenth centuries, when the famous *pasticcio* music for operas was made, pasting the "favorite" airs of the period together without rhyme or reason.

The apprenticeship is slow. New art forms are not made in a day. The function of the true composer for the cinema is not that of superimposing music on the scenes to the order of the director of the production. He should have a conception of the cinematographic work as a whole, and of music's fulfilling an integral function within it. So that the artist may be capable of such conceptions, he must have a profound understanding of the potentialities of all the cinematographic instruments.

Correlatively, the new physical media of art are valid only when they prove their effective ability to serve the expression of new forms of art, or new ideas and feelings. The composers of the present need large fields of experimentation in which to develop new instrumental aptitudes. It is very natural that, for the moment, no hints of new productions are at hand, since the artists are far from the instruments, while the only ones who know them are the engineers. Piano music would never have existed if the instrument had not come into the hands of artists. Only providing composers and artists with the means of knowing and familiarizing themselves with the new media will pave the way toward the birth of new art forms.

Concerning the particular case of the sound film which we have been mentioning, various distinguished European writers and musicians have said that one of the principal obstacles to the appearance of new forms of cinematographic art is the preponderantly commercial purpose of the producers. If we are to condemn the businessmen, it will not be only because they make use of the cinema, nor can we explain the backwardness of the cinema by the mere fact of its being an article of commerce. Land, water, and air communication are in the same state—so are housing, medicine, and engineering. The book, like the cinema, is a vehicle of ideas and feelings, and is also a material of commerce. Nevertheless, there is constant and accelerated advance in all these branches.

The truth is that the conquest of new forms is slow by nature. Very complex and varied factors cause this.

Cinematographic production responds to a universal demand. Thousands and thousands of stupid films have been made, corresponding to millions and millions of stupid people. Our discontent should not, as a consequence, be with the production of films, but with the stupidity of the public which demands productions of low quality. With this evidence, then, we discover that the problem is not one of cinematographic production, but clearly a social problem of educational nature.

We must note that, in addition to the great semi-literate mass, there are social strata of good ideological quality, with a desire for perfection, and that there has been cinematographic production of undeniable merit corresponding to this social class. Also, we must consider the factor of quantity in cinematographic production. The cinematographic firms have to supply an enormous and growing demand for films, and for this require a special system of production, of division of work, of specialization, which puts them in a position to be able to produce the quantity of films needed to satisfy that demand. The only system of production which guaranteed such results was that known as "standard," for which an adequate personnel was instructed and trained in all departments of the work, in the taking of the picture as well as in the composition of the musical *pasticcio*.

The standard film continues to be the only possible way to produce films in relation to the existing demand. If the producers had used only the musicians, dramatists, writers, artists, and scenic experts of first quality, they would have been limited, surely, to a very small personnel, incapable of producing in sufficient quantity to satisfy the immense demand. Furthermore, so-called works of art have an essential character of uniqueness. *Pelleas and Melisande,* Beethoven's Ninth Symphony, a painting by Leonardo, are special cases, unique in composition and artistic form.

We see that standardized production signifies the establishment and practice of a routine, of procedures, molds, and fixed and general forms. It is therefore contrary to the personal initiative and creative sense of the individual. Furthermore, the educational point of view is what sustains and nurtures what does not exist, but should exist; what the public does not know, but should know. The public asks for what it already knows and likes. Great works have never, on their appearance, contained what the large public already knew. For this reason, great works of art have always surprised the public, and have often offended it. But, as we have seen, the public always evolves more or less rapidly, and finally realizes the validity and beauty of the new work. It is this phenomenon of evolution and transformation which we have called educational. In this sense the greatest art is always educational, as its natural tendency is to bring to the public, to the illiterate or semi-literate masses, what they do not know, understand, or like, so that, finally, through the insistence of their action, that public comes to understand it and finally to take it as its own.

We must, then, distinguish two tendencies or purposes: the commercial—to which standardized production belongs, and the educational—to which the work of art properly speaking belongs. In the first case the success is immediate. In the second it is delayed. In the reality of our present organization the two tendencies coexist, despite the fact that they are contradictory. This is not rare, however, as contradiction is the way in which natural forces live and act.

This clarifies for us the position we must take according to our own purposes, and indicates to us how and in what form we should animate the educational (that is, creative) impulses which will lead toward a new music, toward new forms of human expression. The cultured classes will be truly superior insofar as they tend to produce the constant betterment of humanity as a whole, helping new and wholesome forms and expressions, breaking the dikes of stagnation, and combating the germs of dissolution. Under our present social regime, it is not enough to be convinced of the truth of these ideas, or to accept frankly the responsibility for the realization of these functions. In addition, this responsibility must be backed up with economic force. Who will unite in himself the recognition of his responsibility in the advance of human thought and the necessary economic force? Thought itself opens the way, seeks for itself the way to place the necessary media at its disposal.

It is clear, then, that artistic advance is not a purely subjective process, but a part of the complex of circumstances forming the great sociological picture of the present.

Referring to the radio, those directly responsible are the firms which exploit it commercially. In those cases in which the radio is a state monopoly, the state has an increasing obligation to have sections of electric musical investigation with all the necessary elements.

In regard to the possibilities for a cinematographic production of the highest quality, we can set some general conditions:

I. The conception of the cinematographic work should be made in view of the resources of all the arts concurring in the medium. This presupposes either one man capable of dominating all these arts, or a system of association and effective co-operation among various individuals.

II. The musicians must acquaint themselves with sound-engineering.

III. The cinematographic industry must understand that the production of new types of films will not interfere with the march of standard production, since the success of the new, even though not immediate, contains the possibility of other, later brilliant developments.

The electric apparatus of sound production will facilitate the constant and inevitable development of music in its own unique expression (apart from the cinema or television) and will provide the medium through which music will find new forms of circulation. We have already considered the radio's extraordinary capacity for giving music currency. But the radio will always be a means of hearing music indirectly. For this reason it will never kill the concert, in which we hear music directly in the same place and at the same time it is produced. We enjoy direct audition not only in the concert, but on many occasions. It is worth noting that the great ease and attractiveness of music heard by radio has not affected at all the orchestras and popular ensembles we hear in various popular celebrations, in parks, in festivities of various sorts, and even in our own homes. These forms of musical practice have been bettered and fortified, far from having given proofs of decadence, by the success of the radio.

Music in the open air has an enormous place in tropical countries, and is an unequivocal proof of the legitimacy of its function. In cold countries, Summer concerts are somewhat the same thing. Nevertheless, the natural formalism of concerts (their limited time, given hour, fixed location of the public, etc.) is in strong contrast to the liberty of an orchestra or band playing in a public place for a whole morning or afternoon to a free public listening only to what pleases it, when it wishes to listen, and in the place it likes best. The new electric apparatus of sound production, it is not daring to predict, will bring great new resources to the practice of music in the open air. Or, better, the orchestra of electric instruments will have no limitations with respect to the relation between their sound-capacity and the place in which they play. The problem will be simply to adjust the necessary proportion.

At the present time, the quantity of persons who should be accommodated in an auditorium to hear symphonic music is limited by the sound-capacity of the orchestra. It is impossible to think of doubling the instruments, for this also changes the quality of the music. Reality teaches that the different factors in the development of the musical process are always in proportion: the concert-hall, the orchestra, and symphonic music form an indissoluble unity. Chamber music, the chamber orchestra, and the dimensions of the room in which it plays likewise form a unity. If the characteristics of one of these factors are changed, the unity is necessarily ruined. Concretely, the symphonic music of Wagner or Debussy is music for an ensemble of ninety musicians, which should be heard in a hall with a capacity of three thousand listeners. This is what we call the natural adjustment of the conditions of the process. When the dimensions of the hall increase, the orchestra must be increased in a certain proportion, and the music will then have fatally lost its original characteristics. This, of course, refers to the direct audition of music.

In some very large theaters recently constructed in New York, the orchestra and its electric amplification are heard at the same time. This double, superimposed image is really a deformation in which is heard neither the music in its original purity nor the full advantages of electric transmission. It is an unfortunate compromise. From all this we can conclude that it is unnecessary to break the natural adjustment of the conditions of the process. Wagner never tried to re-write the symphonies of Johann Christian Bach for an orchestra of five flutes, five oboes, five clarinets, four bassoons, eight horns, five trumpets, etc. It is *unnecessary* because nothing prevents us from making a whole new adjustment, in which—if the orchestra has new and greater capacities—the volume of air vibrated shall be greater and the music entirely new. This is, I believe, the best solution.

It will be *necessary* only if our generation cannot arrive at the point of creating the new musical forms related to the new resources. In that case we shall have to be satisfied with using the new apparatus and electric wired transmission merely to give a new treatment to old music. With the electric apparatus of sound production we shall be able to perform music adequate to the enormous theaters of our epoch and to places in the open air, so that the public will get, in effect, the direct audition of the instruments producing the sound.

The collaboration of engineers and musicians should produce, in a few years, a material appropriate and practical for huge electric musical performances. The incredible harmony of timbres, in which the perfect gradation of coloring is obtained; the evaluating of the intensity of the planes which produce an effective perspective of sound; the articulation of the most complex rhythms; the most delicate and varied melodization—all this will be achieved through the electric media of sound production.

It is not necessary to predict the medium of instrumental performance. It may be direct human performance or operation by rolls or other mechanical media. Long experimentation will make this clear.

It will be well to say that these new developments do not appear as a sign that previous stages are necessarily exhausted. The symphonic music of today is far from being exhausted. But the fact that we can still do much with our present symphony orchestra does not mean that we cannot do more with the new electric one. It is equally true that it is not impossible to write music for non-chromatic horns and trumpets—for virginals and violas d'amore—for the *aulos* and Greek lyres.

It is evident that an instrumental tradition of seven thousand years is not going to be broken by one blow. We are not trying to break anything—we are trying to make what does not yet exist. With the education those seventy centuries (and uncounted prehistoric centuries) have given us, we have become capable of giving form to musical concepts which are the antecedents of the new. Our epoch of electricity shows the way to immense new developments in the forms and media of art. Great and important for us, the men of today; small and innocent for the men of tomorrow, for those of only a few hundred years from now.

But someone will ask on seeing that the pages of this little book are coming to an end, "What will this new music be like?" In reality, we know nothing about it. This book lacks some paragraphs dealing with the aesthetic of the new music. It certainly contains no descriptions of the music of the future— that is true.

It seems to me that all that is sensible is to speak of the constantly greater use of the media at our disposal. Our optimistic position is that, if the resources of nature have no limitations, the intelligence, imagination, and sensibility of men are also infinite. To foresee the new musical expressions or the aesthetic of a filmed music drama—the effective and balanced synthesis of all the concurring arts—would be equivalent to being able to produce them. Each work of art is a particular case of solving the always complex problem of human expression. I do not believe in futurism. I believe only in the present. Only he who is able to create it can establish the orientations of a non-existent art. It will be preferable to attempt that creation.